COLLEGE UNRANKED

COLLEGE UNRANKED

Affirming Educational Values In College Admissions

edited by Lloyd Thacker

THE EDUCATION CONSERVANCY

To my mother and father, and my wife, Lori.

Such love.

*"Not everything that can be counted counts,
and not everything that counts can be counted."*
Albert Einstein

Contents

Preface

My education began in my father's lap, a lap shared with three siblings, all girls. Here, in this crowded nest of pajama-clad fledglings, imaginations sputtered, flourished, and under the influence of reading, were secured permanently as wings for living.

One long-ago evening, after climbing up and grabbing on, my sisters and I began another literary excursion. "The Congo," a poem by Vachel Lindsay, was one of my father's favorites. That night, we followed his voice into "The Congo."

"…boomlay, boomlay, boomlay boom." Such immediate forte pulse drove my father's energy down against the floor. As both feet pushed hard, his every instinct strained to accelerate that rocking chair into the danger zone of Lindsay's hypnotic rhythm. Suddenly, with a time-punctuating crack, the chair collapsed, spilling father and children backwards in a tangled heap onto the kitchen floor.

Learning reigned supreme in our home. It was celebrated naturally, without fanfare, measurement, comparison, or justification. Sometimes we learned better than we ate; we definitely learned while we ate; we especially learned about what we were eating. Nothing escaped the educational radar screen, in part, I suspect, because we did not have that other kind of screen. And so it was to be with many of the experiences my parents afforded me, during a childhood which I can only recall as blissful.

With my relationship to learning so intimately and joyfully established, I applied to college. Interested in science and oceanography, aware of a college that had these programs, and knowing that I qualified for financial aid, I rolled up my sleeves and was off—thrilled by the prospect of making learning happen in a new environment. In college, the pains, the joys, the discoveries, the disappointments, the friends, the growth, and the many etceteras contributed to the most rewarding and transformative years of my life. Though I may have rocked (sometimes recklessly) to learning's various rhythms, college for the most part was a lot like balancing on my father's knee: a reference point for life.

The years passed. In 1981 I was a young, idealistic admissions officer working at the University of Southern California. A projected demographic shift had caused uncertainty about maintaining enrollments, and one of my tasks was to craft a remedy in the form of a strategic marketing plan. Heretofore, marketing had been considered foreign to college admissions—unseemly, even inappropriate. But ideas borrowed from the private sector had begun to take root in times of declining numbers of students. This movement intrigued me. Marketing liberal education? From the beginning, something did not smell right. Somehow I sensed an impending clash between the values of liberal education and the forces of economic pragmatism.

Today, despite the best intentions of so many fine admission officers, deans, and high school counselors, college admissions has become a multi-billion dollar industry unduly influenced by businesses external to the education community. My job has changed as well. Having followed a personal interest in education to the counseling side of admissions, I now look into the eyes of college-bound students. The fear and anxiety I see expressed seem alien to my own educational sensibilities; I consider these reactions indictments of commercialism's expanding influence in admissions. This radical commercial transformation has proceeded with unusual rapidity and force—a parasite in a most unlikely host, extracting resources in the name of education, delivering no tangible educational rewards, and undermining many traditional educational values. While the beneficiaries have become enriched, the stewardship of student needs has been forsaken. Recently, one of my favorite students said as he stood trembling in my office, "The commercialization of college admissions is so powerful that it has me doing things that are completely contrary to my values; it is driving me crazy!" What a tribute to commercialism's success; what an indictment of its impropriety; what a dire call for corrective action.

Scattered widely across the landscape of college admissions, utterances of concern have been emerging. Would providing a stage for these concerns to be heard make sense? Who would be attracted? What messages would this collective conscience bring? How loudly would it speak, and to whom? For me, these and other questions constituted an irresistible, hopeful, and undeniable challenge.

An impressive group of university officials eagerly answered my invitation to submit essays. Indeed, the educational needs of students, cornered by commercialism, have summoned unusual attention. These essays represent personal investments and insights beyond my expectations—voices resonating earnestly, with singular educational resolve, a seminal collective response. I feel compelled to provide a vehicle for their important messages, all the while reverently aware of the rocking chair's fragility.

Introduction

"If I don't get into a top-ranked college, I'll have to go to a public university, I will be stupid," says a high school junior to her counselor.

"We are all lying in order to improve our college's rank," confesses the dean of a highly ranked college.

"So, you are only a fourteen?" exclaims a disappointed mom to her son after asking the counselor where, on a list of ranked colleges, her son might be admitted.

Welcome to the marketplace of college admissions, an increasingly unwelcoming place for the intellectually curious, the ethical, the visionary, the compassionate, and the hopeful: students eager to build an education and a world. For them, gaining admission to college has been reduced to a game to be played, and education reduced to a prize that must be won. And for the parents of these students, driven to gain every advantage for their children—what a costly, exasperating, and inherently unproductive and shameful process it has become!

On the other side of the admissions desk, deans struggle—often with their own consciences—to land the most desirable, though not necessarily the most qualified, students using strategies that have recently been considered inappropriate for education. Ultimately responsible, college presidents confront a most self-revealing challenge: how to create an educational vision for their institutions while crafting an institutional image according to externally defined criteria—those determined by the "ranksters." Tragically, the educational norms that have helped shape and distinguish higher education are under siege.

Commercialism's intrusion into college admission has transformed a uniquely American educational experience into a problematic American commercial exercise. This rapid commercialization, led by *U.S.News & World Report's* rankings, the domination by the College Board (SAT, test prep, application prep, private tutorials, scholarship services, AP exams, enrollment management, etc.), certain press entities, and the billion dollar college and student marketing and consultant industry, has turned college into mere brand. It has redefined students and their parents as customers and has transformed a key, lifetime passage into a most troubling high-stakes game. Policies, practices, and behaviors once formulated according to educational criteria have been supplanted by private sector mechanisms. These mechanisms do not resonate with the educational sensibilities of students, parents, counselors, deans, and presidents. As a result, fear, anxiety, myth, secrecy, false precision, hype, and educational irrationality characterize the admissions landscape. While billions of dollars have been made by the industries and practices involved in this transformation, the associated educational costs are incalculable.

The American goal used to be "go to college"; now it's "go to the right college." This transformation has proceeded with such rapidity and magnitude that only recently has the mainstream press begun to reflect on its impact. Now, not a day goes by without a story on college admission and its related developments appearing in a major news publication. The new SAT, Affirmative Action, Early Decision, preferential admissions, FBI investigation of one university hacking into another's admissions records, scholarships for the wealthy, scholarship scams, athletic agents, college branding...these and other topics have come to dominate the new media darling, college admissions.

Consider the following titles of articles that have recently appeared in major national news publications: "Buying Your Way into College," "How Colleges Reject Top Applicants and Boost Their Status," "The Great College Hustle," "The Early Decision Racket," "The College Chase," "Eyes on the College Prize," "The Tricks of the Trade," "The Quest for Students," "How I Spent Summer Vacation: At Getting into College Camp." Notice that key words in these titles, which are words more often associated with something other than serving education, include "tricks," "hustle," "racket," "chase," and "prize." In the midst of this new media attention, certain issues are beginning to command national public interest:

- **The use of financial aid.** A radical shift has occurred in the use of financial aid—from meeting student need to serving institutional self-interest, as exhibited by the three-fold increase in scholarship money awarded during the past five years while need-based aid has declined. "It used to be that providing aid was a charitable operation," said Michael McPherson, former president of Macalester College and a higher education economist. "Now it's an investment, like brand management" (*The New York Times,* as quoted in *The American Prospect,* October 7, 2002). There is growing concern that the increasing use of financial aid for strategic purposes (increasing rank and maximizing revenue) is violating equity principles traditionally associated with education. "The whole issue of access for low income folks got lost in the dust," says an education economist in *The New York Times* (May 2, 2002). An Educational Testing Service study of the 146 most selective colleges concluded that 3 percent of the students came from the nation's bottom economic quartile while 74 percent hail from the top quartile (*The Nation*, October 13, 2003).

- **The influence of outside agencies**. The rise and influence of the billion-dollar Enrollment Management Consulting industry, which specializes in packaging and branding colleges according to strict bottom-line rationality and strategizing, is raising questions about what values and principles should determine college admission policy. A survey by the National Association for College Admission Counseling revealed that 74 percent of colleges surveyed had invested in an image overhaul during 2002 - 2003. It is safe to say that most, if not all, employed private consulting services.

- **The redirecting of institutional funds in appealing to students as customers.** There has been a reported 270 - 300 percent four-year average increase in college marketing budgets committed to attracting and enrolling students since 1999. Thirty-four percent of colleges now spend more than $2,200 to attract and enroll each student. The construction of posh living centers, student health centers, and on-campus restaurants has had a whopping budgetary impact, averaging $3,000 - $5,000 per student (*The Wall Street Journal*, November 10, 2000).

• **The advent of the student agency industries.** Relatively new additions to the college admission process include the college counselor industry, a group of largely self-proclaimed experts in securing further advantage for those who can afford their services; scholarship search services; athletic agents; and learning development specialists. These services rake in more than $500 million annually while providing services of often questionable educational value. The Scholarship Fraud Protection Act of 2000 made it easier for individuals to report scholarship fraud, yet in 2001, 350,000 students and families lost more than $5 million to scholarship fraud; the following year that amount rose to $22 million (*NACAC Journal*, January 2001).

• **The success of marketing prestige and popularity as important educational criteria** has contributed to a dramatic increase in freshman applications, with a disproportionate number of these applications going to elite colleges. According to UCLA's Higher Education Research Institute, the portion of students submitting four or more applications increased from 15 percent in 1969 to 38 percent in 2000. In 2003, 787 guidance counselors responding to a survey conducted by The National Association for College Admission Counseling reported that 74 percent of their students had applied to four or more colleges. Commenting on this increase, Lee Stetson, Dean of Admission at the University of Pennsylvania, observed, "80 percent of the extra applications are going to 20 percent of the schools" (*The Atlantic Monthly*, November 2003).

- **The increase in gamesmanship, falsification of data, and negotiation.** The National Association for College Admission Counseling noted that 26 percent of colleges surveyed during 2002 - 2003 reported an increase in unethical admission practices.

- **The "corporatization" of The College Board and its increasing domination of standardized testing.** The College Board raised $24 million in venture capital to create CollegeBoard.com in a failing effort to compete with other purveyors of college prep services and materials. This attempt at a non-profit/for-profit marriage continues to raise questions about the College Board's non profit status and credibility.

- **The test prep industry.** Demonstrating that test prep can increase college options for those who can afford these services, this billion-dollar industry (24 percent growth during 2002) is now owned and controlled by media giants. At the same time, colleges are paying more attention to test scores in selecting students, mainly to increase college rank.

As the smoldering discussion about college admission practices ignites, values of cultural significance are being called into question. Twenty-five years ago, college admission was a fairly low profile, low impact activity involving students and admission counselors. Today it has all the characteristics of big business: high stakes, emotionally charged, lots of money, media worthy, and politically popular.

As a result, participants in the system have been rendered both consumers and products. For parents and students, this means learning to "market" and "package" themselves and their achievements to colleges through the use of SAT prep programs, essay-writing tutorials, college application summer prep camps, college consultants, and scholarship search agencies. For high school counselors, this requires doing all they can to deliver parents and students the coveted admission-to-the-first-choice-college prize. All the while, college presidents and admission deans must market their school's reputation, image, and brand to parents and students, as they would an automobile, to secure the most "desirable" students and the highest rankings.

It has been suggested that college admission has merely gone the way of law and medicine over the past few years—that the same "cultural" influences affecting these "industries" are inevitable, maybe even beneficial. Concurrently, there is growing acknowledgement that commercialism and education may not blend well. Many sense that business precepts have limited use in the realm of education: that what is good for business is not necessarily appropriate for education.

Encouragingly, some of the strongest criticism of the rankings and GREATEST CONCERN ABOUT commercialism's influence in college admissions has emerged from leaders of those institutions that have benefited from such practices:

Lee Bollinger, president of Columbia University, College Board Forum keynote address, January 31, 2002:

> "The more fundamental issue facing education is the seemingly endlessly rising sense of competition—or a particular kind of competition—among applicants and students and among selective colleges and universities."

> "And the problem—the large and fundamental problem—is that we are at risk of it all seeming, and becoming, more and more a game. What matters is less the education and more the brand."

> "The tentacles of this way of thinking have the potential to reach into every corner of our general understanding of intellectual and artistic life. Not all forms of competition are equal, and there will always be the risk of a downward spiral in an atmosphere that values the wrong things. We must never forget that much of what makes colleges and universities special, and over the long run socially important, is both highly fragile and counter-intuitive in a democratic and a free market system."

Gerhard Casper, former president of Stanford University, from an unpublished letter to *U.S.News & World Report*, September 1996:

> "As the president of a university that is among the top-ranked universities, I hope I have the standing to convince you that much about these rankings— particularly their specious formulas and spurious precision—is utterly misleading."

Richard R. Beeman, dean of the College of Arts and Sciences, University of Pennsylvania, *The New York Times*, September 18, 2002:

> "Rankings both underestimate the amount of work it takes to get a college education and overestimate the importance of a university's prestige in that process. In that way, they may do considerable harm to the educational enterprise itself."

Robert Reich, former Secretary of Labor, current professor at Brandeis University, *The Chronicle of Higher Education*, June 2003:

> "Many colleges have sharpened their business practices by confusing what is good for business with what is good for education. Nationally, the demand for college educated people is outpacing supply, yet the college going rate for the bottom income quartile is decreasing while the top quartile grows to approach three times that of the bottom quartile. The increasing competition to be selective and to be selected has exacerbated the widening inequalities that are raising the stakes in the first place."

Derek Bok, author and former president of Harvard University, *Universities in the Marketplace*, 2004:

> "Competition succeeds only to the extent that customers, judges, or other trusted sources can define success in some legitimate way in order to establish a standard and reward those who best achieve it. In education, at least at the university level, this ability is lacking."

Nicholas Lemann, author and professor at Columbia University, *The Big Test,* 2000:

> "Americans' preoccupation with admission to selective colleges has gone past the bounds of rationality. The culture of frenzy surrounding admissions is destructive and anti-democratic; it warps the sensibilities and distorts the education of the millions of people whose lives it is supposed to serve"

These collective concerns call for solutions to the increasing disconnect between educational purposes and admission practices. While there is growing acknowledgement that something is dreadfully wrong, an appropriate response has yet to emerge. What can be done? Are commercial forces so successful as to repress educational conscience? Certainly education deserves to fight back.

The essays in this book respond to this crisis. They represent a conscience which is emerging among college officials and admission professionals. They speak directly to students, parents, colleges, and other groups involved in college admissions. They criticize, implore, advocate, and advise, all with one goal in mind: serving the educational needs of students. Collectively they offer hope and promise for the future of higher education.

Before turning to the essays, it is helpful for the reader to understand "studenthood," a concept I have developed while watching students, parents, teachers, and admission officials struggle with aspects of commercialism in college admissions. Most educators view education as a process—one in which the role of the student in "making education happen" is essential. Studenthood refers to those qualities that equip a student to make education happen, to engage learning as a process. Curiosity, self-discipline, effort, imagination, intellectual verve, sense of wonder, willingness to try new things, empathy, open-mindedness, civility, tolerance for ambiguity—these are some of the qualities that define and give value to being a student. These are the same qualities that colleges say they seek in admitting prospective students. Yet these are qualities that the commercialization of college admission has done more to betray and repress than to serve, as they are not measurable, and cannot be factored into college rankings and other attempts to quantify education. By giving these qualities a name, studenthood, I am suggesting that they make up a vital educational resource: a resource being abused in the current college admission environment, a resource which needs to be reclaimed from the clutches of commercialism. When embraced this way, studenthood helps us stay focused on the values and value associated with education, while responding to the challenges of commercialism.

Education is a process, not a product. Students are learners, not customers.

The benefits and predictors of good education are knowable, yet virtually impossible to measure.

Rankings oversimplify and mislead.

A student's intellectual skills and attitude about learning are more important than where that student goes to college.

Educational values are best served by admission practices that are consistent with these values.

College admissions should be part of an educational process directed toward student autonomy and intellectual maturity.

Colleges can be assessed, but not ranked. Students can be evaluated, but not measured.

Students' thoughts, ideas, and passions are worthy to be engaged and handled with utmost care.

The Advisory Board of the Education Conservancy

College Recruitment Night

Kim Stafford
Director, Northwest Writing Institute, Lewis & Clark College

"She does not know. And no college can know. The path of not knowing—yet—that is what college is for."

If you are parent to a teenager counting down the years at home, you may know where I stand. In this carpeted hotel salon with darkened chandeliers, a panel of pert admissions reps from eight exclusive colleges take turns flashing slides at a packed house of high school students and their parents. On the screen, we glimpse a class of bright young faces in a dark-paneled room, the professor's hands raised to choreograph an idea, then a soccer player leaps in gold sunlight, and then a student with furrowed brow holds up a tangle of equipment beside her bespeckled professor—an artifact of their collaborative research in some advanced delineation of DNA. The slides click along, and from the podium we hear about faculty-student ratios, financial aid, distinctive student activities, and a litany of academic excellences. One recruiter gets off a zinger: "Our endowment is approaching a billion dollars." Another brags of campus proximity to New York City: "Our history seminars are regularly taught at the Metropolitan Museum of Art." Another extols the virtues of a campus with rural isolation...the self-directed path of inquiry...the student-monitored honor system...technology to die for. Successful graduates have become sound bytes in each college's collective reputation against which our children—should they apply—will be measured. We hear bragged each college's graduate stable: names of actors, writers, senators...the secretary-general of the United Nations.

Tonight, my sixteen year old daughter is seated among the throng, and I am standing in the back, holding the baby. The room is resonant with hype and hope, and with a sizzling electric fear, for the stakes for everyone are very high. Suddenly, a young man bolts

11

past me for the rear door. Halfway across the carpeted arena, he clutches his throat and vomits in the dark—with a moan and a gurgle his expectation and terror escaping him. He staggers alone, and then slinks away into the lobby. The door closes behind him, and the show goes on.

I follow him out, trying to find someone to help me spread a towel over the mess. In the basement lobby, I rock back and forth to soothe the baby. The young man has disappeared, and I try to remember what he must feel, as I reach back thirty years to my own days of applying for what I hoped would be passage through the doorway of a prestigious college to some vague prophecy of success. I remember how nothing worked out exactly as I had planned: Stanford rejected my application, and I attended the University of Oregon for twelve years, earning a Ph.D. in Medieval Literature. Who could have predicted that? Yet here I am, doing what I want to do. I teach at a college myself (where we brag about our own Rhodes Scholar this year); I do some writing; and I have a wife, a baby, and a sixteen year old daughter I love.

The lobby is bright, but no one is there to help. As I return to the dark room, as the door hushes closed behind me, and the speaker's confident voice reaches to envelope me—"We accept one applicant in twelve..."—suddenly I feel a place in my mind for a message different from the articulate brag I am hearing. It is a place for the mystery of learning, not mere excellence of achievement. I long for recognition of the treasure of a young life, not a test for intellectual sufficiency in an applicant. I want for my daughter not college per se, not excellence or competition or "Your Future at Our School," but some acknowledgement of the brief, rich drama of this particular handful of years in a young person's life. Who will speak to that?

In the darkness before me I try to find my daughter's head among the grid of silhouettes against the screen. I can't pick her out. The slides go on, and the voice of yet another admissions recruiter proclaims her college's virtues: "Our college consistently produces students who are..." (and a list of characteristics follows). "Consistently"? "Produces"? Is this a factory of intellection?

I find myself staring into the darkened rows of listeners before me, and trying to send a message to my girl who soon will be gone from home. I want someone at the podium to step aside from loyalty to a college, and be loyal instead to my child, loyal to the drama of her journey. I want someone to accompany her with words something like these....

Let's say you are on your way to my college—that we are that lucky. The morning has come, and you have packed a big suitcase. You look around the room at things you will leave—a tattered first book, an animal with a name, a dried corsage, and that window where all your mornings came to wake you. The leaves outside shiver once, then hold steady.

By the front door you say good-by to your parents. The moment you turn away—there or at some station or airport—you feel it in your bones: never again to meet on these terms. You have walked out of one life, and into another. You are afraid, and excited—on your way.

From there to here—from home to a college campus—you experience an accelerated beginning into a future that belongs only to you. You know direction like a river knows it, urgent and inevitable. When you arrive on campus, everything courts you feverishly—people and ideas you have never met, lovers sweet and cruel, great books, alcohol, intoxicating subjects, despair, joy, good friends, professors eager to recruit you to their cause. You are alone, and in wonderful company, and then alone, and in dangerous company, and then alone again. How to sort it out? Late some night you stare at a book you cannot understand, for all your trying, and you feel you can't prevail. The light in your room shines on everything, but illuminates nothing. Your mind falters, your spirit withers. And that night, empowered by your parents' gifts, your years in school, and the secret virtues of your character, you have no choice but to go on.

Some power that is in you now will help you then.

No college can anticipate fully what treasures you may bring to their community. We can only guess. Your application and our admission process is a guess—a good guess, probably, but a mysterious path, finally. For the treasure of who you are does belong somewhere. Maybe it is with my college, or one of the colleges represented here. Maybe with another. And maybe with none. Colleges like to think they have the power to "produce" great graduates, like factories of character. But we can't do that. Your high school, for all its virtues, could not create you, only accompany you on a part of your journey, and we are similar. With luck, we can be a place where good faculty, enriching traditions, and a sequence of unpredictable moments of deep learning may give you courage—may invite you to grow from the unique life you bring to our ground toward something neither you nor I can now imagine.

If you apply and we don't accept you, no one has failed. If we accept you and we don't turn out to be the best place for you, no one has failed. The real thing is you—your life of learning that can be nourished, stunted, accelerated, re-directed, but never stopped. This life belongs to you. We can only promise gifts of our own to meet the gifts you bring. You may share with us a part in this very old story: you the magic traveler, and we the castle with an open door. You bring us life.

My eyes come back to focus on the screen: snowy mountains behind a college dormitory. One of the Claremont schools. A list of successful graduates, their achievements. My wife has lifted the baby from my arms, and carried him away. The young man has returned, apparently recovered, alert, and ready. He hesitates at the door to get his bearings, then strides forward. Somewhere in the dark, my daughter is keeping her soul alive in a busy world. I do not know what she will do. She does not know. And no college can know. This path of not knowing—yet—this is what college is for.

Standing in the dark, I give up my treasure to this mystery.

Let Them Be Students

William M. Shain
Dean of Undergraduate Admissions, Vanderbilt University

"...if students were only left more to their own devices, the process would proceed more appropriately...it is the intervention of adults that has added layers of competition and anxiety..."

More that fifty years ago, a British actor, singer, and song writer named Noel Coward created a song entitled "What's Going to Happen to the Children (When There Aren't Any More Grown-Ups)?" As I reflect on the current state of college admissions in the U.S., this song keeps coming to mind, because I find myself thinking that if students were only left more to their own devices, the process would proceed more appropriately. It is the intervention of adults that has added layers of competition and anxiety well beyond what is intrinsic to any competitive selection process. Journalists, university administrators, parents, counselors, and even admission officers all contribute to painful tendencies which, at their worst, can change the college search process from one of matching a student to an appropriate institution, to a look-alike for a television reality show with a total emphasis on winning.

It is too easy, of course, simply to catalog the most distressing instances in a process involving millions of individuals in each recruitment cycle. It is critical to remember that the vast majority of people involved in pursuing, producing, or commenting upon the college admission process are caring, decent individuals earnestly trying to do what is right. However, as in any other field, excessive behaviors and ethical lapses can cast an entire process into disrepute. Because of the harmful impact they have on students, these poor choices sadden me, and will represent the focus of my comments.

When I started work in college admissions at Princeton University more than twenty-five years ago, the work was mostly fun and the pace (aside from file-reading season) was often gentle. There was room, even at Princeton, for kids who just seemed interesting even if their credentials were not spectacular. The work was generally personal, almost totally outside the public eye, and obsessed with fairness.

Things changed permanently in the 1980s. I have always believed the change resulted from the first decline since World War II in the number of students graduating from high school. Colleges began to realize that they would have to work harder and more competitively to maintain the size and academic quality of their entering classes. Ever more transformational was the onset of media coverage of the field of college admissions. There was no turning back from either of these watersheds.

I have always enjoyed most contacts with the media. My father was a journalist and I grew up in a home that received a staggering seven daily newspapers. However, over time I have become disappointed with much of the coverage of college admissions, especially in the last decade or so. Too many stories are sensationalized and serve only to scare students (and their parents) approaching the college process. Perhaps that is inevitable, since I have trouble seeing admissions as all that newsworthy. Stories focus disproportionately on a handful of the most selective institutions, when no more than about 50 of the more than 3,000 colleges and universities in the U.S. actually admit fewer students than they turn down. And guides with ratings have proliferated, with criteria that appear to have been selected because information is easily available (rather than important) and evaluated by a methodology that is frequently flawed and even more often not fully explained.

The result, too often, is to shift a student's college search process from finding a school that matches academic and personal needs to gaining access to institutions approved of by external sources. As admission to the most competitive schools becomes more difficult, anxiety leads students to apply to more of these schools.

Applications to the most selective institutions each year rise far faster than any increase in the number of students applying to college. Under these conditions, it is no surprise that families begin to approach the process in disappointing and even self-defeating ways.

In particular, upper income parents on too many occasions come to see the college choice process in terms of winning instead of matching their child to institutions where they are likely to be happiest and most successful. College admission in many communities, especially in the Boston-Washington corridor, can too easily take on a Darwinian flavor of survival of the fittest. Witness the following unfortunate parental approaches: (1) Pressuring students—and secondary schools—to schedule courses at a level of rigor beyond their ability or appropriate comfort zone; (2) Excessive focus on all activity choices—for the student and for the family—in terms of the college process. School activities are chosen based on perceived college preferences. Worst of all, summer activities are centered on the study of employment options which admissions offices are believed to prefer. I have never met an admission officer who maintained any hierarchy of values for summer activities. The point is what the student got out of the summer, not the prestige of the options parental influence is able to create. I have seen students gain far more from working as a bagger in a supermarket than studying overseas, for instance. And because university summer courses are rarely taught by full-time faculty, grades in these courses carry minimal weight in admission process, certainly far less than grades indicated on the student's secondary school transcript.

It is all too easy for me to advise parents on an alternative approach, since I have not raised children. However, some approaches seem obvious. First of all, before ever creating a college list, families should spend more time developing criteria based on their values and the student's academic and personal preferences. Second, admissions selectivity is a poor criterion. It measures market appeal and the effectiveness of promotion rather than the quality of education. Of course, academic differences are likely between two schools with admission rates of, say, 90 percent and 20 percent. But I question whether a 20 point difference in admission rates creates a valid assumption concerning academic quality. Third, parents need to be realistic about competition for admission to the most popular schools. I talked a few weeks ago with a counselor at an exceptional public school in Westchester County, N.Y., who asked if Vanderbilt would consider a late application from a student with a 4.0 average and 1440 SATs who had not been admitted anywhere. This superior student had undoubtedly aimed too high and failed to create a balanced and realistic application protocol. Parents must heed counselors when they warn against an application or overall posture based on an unrealistic selectivity match, and must do up-to-date research on admission processes since annual changes can be significant. (Vanderbilt's freshman admission rate, for instance, has dropped from 60 percent to 40 percent in five years.) Finally, parents must resist the tendency to have students apply to too many institutions. Applications take a great deal of time, and, to have impact, must be based on a relationship with each institution. Not every student can visit before admission decisions are mailed, but students should have many of the other possible contacts with institutions: meetings with representatives at college fairs and/or high school visits, phone or other contact with admission staff and alumni, and application materials which reflect awareness of the distinctiveness of the college involved.

University administrators too often also contribute negatively to the college choice process. The most common, and most understandable, way this happens is through excessive concern with admission statistics. Up to a point, it is appropriate to aspire to each entering class possessing greater academic talent than its predecessor. However, I worry about there being no limit to this quest. Certainly, a 20 percent admission rate is not necessary to have an entering class of students talented enough to excite intellectually both a top faculty and each other. I have long believed that below a 30 percent admission rate, a class is not really getting better. Rather, test scores rise from the very high to the stratospheric, and more valedictorians are denied admission. To my knowledge, no one has ever documented that this brings any improvement in the quality of intellectual discourse on campus. Institutions do not change as rapidly as do guidebook ratings. Unfortunately, the problem is compounded by the practice of bond-raters for institutional borrowing to rely heavily on freshman admission statistics, using the Ivy League as a prototype. Institutions fail or default on financial obligations very infrequently, and I find the reliance on admissions data for these purposes to be hard to justify beyond extreme situations.

I have worked for three institutions and seven chief executive officers, and in every case have been gratified by the concern from the top down for the fairness of the admission process. It must be remembered that admission decisions represent an art rather than a science, and transcend mere number crunching. Indeed, this holistic approach is one of the hallmarks separating American higher education from most of the rest of the world's selection systems. In addition, each institution appropriately creates its own design for a demographic utopia. Students with special non-academic or academic talents or particular family backgrounds will vary in their appeal from institution to institution. However, the practices of a few highly selective institutions—and some journalistic coverage, especially in *The Wall Street Journal*—has unfortunately called into question the fundamental fairness of the entire system. Admission offices are vigilant to make as many decisions as possible on the same basis for all candidates, and consistently resist pressures from other university constituencies to award excessive places in an entering class to candidates based on financial, ethnic, athletic, or other "special" considerations. The result at all but perhaps a handful of selective institutions is a healthy dialectic that almost always is fair to both candidates and institutional needs.

It is, of course, college guidance counselors who bear a particularly heavy burden as the admission process becomes more intense and students face ever-greater pressures. I am impressed more frequently than I can count with the integrity, aggressive search for current information, and genuine concern for each student shown by the vast majority of college counselors with whom I interact. However, even these good people on occasion maintain practices that I think are to the detriment of their counselees. (1) The increase in selectivity presented by many universities appropriately leads counselors to warn students about diminishing chances for admission at many popular institutions. Counseling related to selectivity, though, often errs on the other end. It is common practice to suggest students apply to at least one "reach" school, one where admission is a long shot. I have never seen the sense in this, in that selectivity has no intrinsic relation to a match for the student. A "reach" school may, indeed, be an appropriate option for a given student, but because it matches the student's criteria, *not* merely because it is hard to get into. (2) In fear of lock-step use of class rank in the admission process, many of the most competitive secondary schools have discontinued reporting class rank in the college admission process. In place of this, schools typically provide grade distribution information, so that a college can estimate how well a student has performed in academic course work. This presents no difficulty in an admission process, and in especially competitive schools may be an appropriate approach. However, lately a number of schools have taken this further, providing no information at all about what their grades mean in context. An admission office can calculate, say, that a student has a 3.25 grade point average, but has no idea if a 3.25 is a strong, average, or weak performance in the particular school. (Median grade point averages can vary between approximately 2.8 and 3.5 from school to school.) The result of this practice is to make test scores carry far greater weight, since comparative academic achievement is not available. In addition, in Vanderbilt's admission process, we presume in the absence of other information that the school has a very high grading curve —the highest we find any school reporting—so the practice will serve to disadvantage a student if, indeed, the grading curve has a median below, say, 3.50.

Finally, it is appropriate for admission officers to reflect on the extent to which our own practices can make it more difficult for a student to conduct their college process in the most enjoyable and effective manner. As with college counselors, admission officers choose their profession in large part because they want to serve students, as well as their own institution. I am frequently touched by the kindness and sensitivity I see among my Vanderbilt admission colleagues and admission officers at a host of other institutions. Still, if we wish to be as "client-centered" as circumstances would allow, a few fairly widespread practices might well be questioned.

I am concerned, to begin with, that we often go past mere recruitment to almost browbeating students with excessive contact. I have no way of knowing how much is too much, but weekly mailings for the last two years of high school would seem not to be a service to students. The result is an "admissions arms race" where every school feels pressure to keep up with the competition. It must be borne in mind that every dollar spent on recruitment is a dollar not spent on teaching and facilities, and we must always strive to balance these competing institutional financial priorities. In addition, excessive recruitment, especially if students are not carefully pre-screened, can too easily create an inappropriate expectation of admission, and, in so doing, dangerously distort a student's college choice process.

I worry, too, that admission offices are often less than candid about several critical issues: the threshold for admission, the impact of choosing an Early Decision process, and the intersection of financial aid requests and admission decisions. First, admission thresholds. In an era when it is harder to gain admission to many schools, it can also seem hard to find out what one's chances for admission really are. The most selective institutions too often seem to downplay how difficult it is to get in, perhaps in the interest of keeping application numbers (and, consequently, selectivity and both admissions and bond ratings) high. Few of these schools make easily available on their websites and elsewhere information that makes it clear how very hard it really is to gain admission. On the other hand, schools with less competitive admissions profiles often exaggerate their selectivity in communication with prospective students, especially in presentations at high schools and to campus visitors. Whenever we are less than candid about selectivity thresholds with the public, we can lead a student to a dangerously ill-informed application posture.

Early Decision processes these days get more attention than is perhaps appropriate, but a few comments still seem appropriate. Available information strongly suggests that thresholds for admission under a binding early decision process are lower at almost all institutions that those faced by students applying under the later non-binding deadline. It still seems fine to me that Early Decision students get a modest edge in the application process. Why not, after all, tilt gently towards students who really want to enroll? Given the intensity of today's college choice process, and the far earlier point in time when recruitment now begins, many students are indeed ready to make an informed choice of this type in the early fall of senior year. My preference, however, would be to limit the percentage admitted under early decision plans to perhaps 30 percent of the entering class, unless the early decision pool is actually more competitive, of course, than the rest of the applicant group. (While several schools maintain this is true, it is not a situation I have personally experienced or seen documented.) But it is a reality—and an appropriate one—that schools will make individual choices according to their own sense of ethics and institutional and student needs. What is critical is that processes be explained with honesty. In addition, I am concerned that students not have their application deferred to the regular decision round if they have no chance of serious consideration for admission then. Students who apply early decision tend to cling to their chance of admission, and resist taking other options seriously. That is fine, even touching, as long as the deferred consideration is sincere. If not, it can seriously delay or distort a student's entire college choice process.

Finally, in an era when college costs are in real income the highest they have ever been, we owe it to students and their families to provide accurate information about financial aid processes and how they work. I hear frequently that "no admission process these days is totally need-blind"; that is, that ability to pay is a factor in admission decisions at most universities. I have never been convinced this is true, since all three institutions for which I have worked have indeed been need-blind in admission decisions for students who are eligible for U.S. state and federal aid. In cases where this is not the protocol—or is not maintained for any portion of the admission process (for instance, the waiting list)—fairness to students and their families strongly indicates we must be candid.

All of us interacting with students applying to college would be well-advised to heed the character in the now defunct comic strip "Pogo" who said, "We have met the enemy, and they is us." It is heartening that even in an era of increased moral and financial complexity, the vast majority of admissions communications, decisions, and commentary are intended to be thoughtful and fair. However, college is a vital step towards adulthood for students pursing admission processes. We owe them the best support we can muster, because guiding students is a trust of great consequence. In addition, in preparing students for leadership in our society in the future, it is important that we support them in conducting the college choice process with integrity and genuine reflection. We must never forget that our own actions constitute a critical model for the ethical underpinning we hope America's future leaders will bring to the society of which they will have stewardship a generation from now.

Time Out or Burn Out for the Next Generation

William Fitzsimmons
Dean of Admissions and Financial Aid, Harvard College

Marlyn McGrath Lewis
Director of Admissions, Harvard College

Charles Ducey
Director of the Bureau of Study Counsel, Harvard University

"The pressures placed on many children—probably have the unintended effect of delaying a child's finding herself and succeeding on her own terms."

College admissions officers, especially those who admitted the parents of today's applicants, have an unusual vantage point from which to observe changes from one generation to the next. Many of us are concerned that the pressures on today's students seem far more intense than those placed on previous generations. College admission—the chance to position oneself for "success" through the acquisition of the "right" college degree—looms large for increasing numbers of students. Particularly because selective colleges are perceived to be part of the problem, we want to do everything possible to help the students we enroll make the most of their opportunities, avoiding the much-reported "burnout" phenomenon that can keep them from reaching their full potential.

Of course, the quest for college admission is only one aspect of a much larger syndrome driving many students today. Stories about the latest twenty-something ".com" multimillionaires, the astronomical salaries for athletes and pop-music stars, and the often staggering compensation packages for CEOs only stimulate the frenzied search for the brass ring. More than ever, students (and their parents) seek to emulate those who win the "top prizes" and the accompanying disproportionate rewards.

From the Cradle On...

The chase for the prize begins early, and some recent reports sound almost hyperbolic. Anecdotes abound of infants serenaded with classical music to enhance their mental powers; toddlers overwhelmed with computers and "educational" toys; "experts" guilt-tripping parents by telling them that their children will be hopelessly behind by age three or four if they don't follow myriad prescribed strategies.

Consultants are paid hundreds, even thousands, of dollars to prepare toddlers for the "all-important" interview and observed play-time that will determine admission to the "right" pre-kindergarten, kindergarten, or primary school—thereby presumably ensuring admission to the right high school, college, graduate school, and so on. The consultant will teach the child to maintain eye contact in the interview and to demonstrate both leadership and sharing during the observed play sequence. The competition for admission to some of the pre-k, kindergarten, and grammar schools can be intense—statistically more difficult (with lower admission rates) than Harvard.

Once in the "right" school, students are pushed along by teachers, by outside tutors and, if they stumble, by learning specialists who will help them approach their studies in the most efficient manner. The school day continues well into the night with structured study time and drills. The pressure can be relentless, even from well-intentioned parents. For the most part, they simply want the best for their children who, they fear, will be left by the wayside by other high achievers.

Sports, music, dance, and other recreational activities used to provide a welcome break, a time to relax and unwind. No more: training for college scholarships—or professional contracts—begins early, even in grammar school. Professional instruction, summer camps, and weekly practice and game schedules consume many hours and nearly all free time. Student and family commuting logistics become byzantine in their complexity. Even "play-time" is often structured and enriched with just the right mix of appropriate playmates and educational activities. Summer vacations have become a thing of the past. The pace of the day and the year allows little time simply "to be a kid"—or, it seems, to develop into a complete human being.

The Middle School/High School Fast Track

By high school, the pressure intensifies. Students start to specialize in one activity even to the exclusion of other pursuits. Athletes, dancers, musicians, and others begin to define themselves by their chosen activity as they try to perfect their new-found talents and identities.

Recently the American Academy of Pediatrics released a policy statement warning of possible physical and psychological damage that can result from specializing in a sport prematurely. For every Tiger Woods success story, there are countless other less happy results. Some students participate in programs that take up as much time as school. Fast-track athletic teams compete or practice most days, with weekend-consuming road games and national or international schedules during summers and vacations. A serious athlete or musician or dancer many change schools for a better athletic program, even moving far away from home to do so, and perhaps to an academically weaker school.

Academic demands also ratchet up, supported by special tutors and the beginnings of SAT prep in middle school. In high school, SAT prep becomes a way of life for some students, with night and weekend sessions. The "right" SAT tutors may command several hundred dollars per hour, and can be engaged to live during the summer at or near their tutees' beach houses. Summer "cram schools" for the SATs are increasingly common, as are summer school sessions at the best prep schools and universities, some beginning in middle school.

The Quest for the Right College

Professional college counselors (either independent or school-based) appear on the scene early, sometimes in middle school, to begin to structure student' academic and extracurricular profiles for entrance to the "right" college. At its best, such advice can be helpful in assessing talents, goals, and making "mid- course corrections" that can make a real difference in students' lives. From a more cynical perspective, such advice steers students toward travel abroad, community service, or other activities solely to enhance college essays or interviews. Such services may command thousands of dollars, and assistance in preparing applications ranges from appropriate to plagiaristic. Videotaped mock college interviews are features of some packages as are guided tours of colleges. One consultant recently announced an array of services that start in ninth grade ("or seventh or eighth grade for no extra charge") for a fee of about $29,000, as well as a service offered separately called Essay Review ("includes brainstorming session and as many revisions as necessary"), which costs $1500. Such services can add to, rather than alleviate, the stress of the normal expectations of school, community, and family life.

The pressure of gaining entrance to the most selective colleges is commonly blamed for much of the stress we observe. But those of us who work in college admissions recognize that college is only one of many destinations in the fast lane. The accumulation of "credentials" simply continues to intensify as the stakes increase. The "right" graduate school looms after college, and the "right" sequence of jobs is next. Such attainments make it possible to live in the "right" kinds of communities and to begin the job of bringing up the following generation, one that might need to vault even higher hurdles.

The Fallout

Faced with the fast pace of growing up today, some students are clearly distressed, engaging in binge drinking and other self-destructive behaviors. Counseling services of secondary schools and colleges have expanded in response to greatly increased demand. It is common to encounter even the most successful students, who have won all the prizes, stepping back and wondering if it was all worth it. Professionals in their thirties and forties—physicians, lawyers, academics, business people, and others—sometimes give the impression that they are dazed survivors of some bewildering life-long boot-camp. Some say they ended up in their profession because of someone else's expectations, or that they simply drifted into it without pausing to think whether they really loved their work. Often they say they missed their youth entirely, never living in the present, always pursuing some ill-defined future goal.

Some Early Remedies

What can we do to help? Fortunately this young fast-track generation itself offers ideas that can reduce stress and prevent burnout. In college application essays and interviews, in conversations and counseling sessions with current college students, and in discussions with alumni/ae, many current students perceive the value of taking time out. Such a "time out" can take many forms. It can be very brief or last for a year or more. It can be structured or unstructured, and directed toward career, academic, or purely personal pursuits. Most fundamentally, it is a time to step back and reflect, to gain perspective on personal values and goals, or to gain needed life experience in a setting separate from and independent of one's accustomed pressures and expectations.

For the years during high school, here is some of the advice students have offered:

> Families should allow for "down-time" during vacations, weekends, and during the week at mealtimes or at any other break in the action. The fabric of family life is already under assault from the demands of parents' increasingly stressful jobs. Parents, some of whom experienced the first wave of fast-lane childhoods themselves, are often distressed by how little uninterrupted free time they have to devote to their children.

> Bring summer back. Summer need not be totally consumed by highly structured programs, such as summer schools, travel programs, or athletic camps. While such activities can be wonderful in many ways, they can also add to stress by

assembling "super peers" who set nearly impossible standards. Activities in which one can develop at one's own pace can be much more pleasant and helpful. An old-fashioned summer job that provides a contrast to the school year or allows students to meet others of differing backgrounds, ages, and life experiences is often invaluable in providing psychological downtime and a window on future possibilities. Students need ample free time to reflect, to recreate (i.e., to "re-create" themselves without the driving pressure to achieve as an influence), and to gather strength for the school year ahead.

Choose a high school (or a college) not simply based on "brand name" or reputation but because it is the best fit. A school with a slower pace or a different academic or extracurricular focus can be a better match for certain students in the long run.

Using the Senior Year

The senior year of high school presents some special challenges and opportunities. Recently the U.S. Department of Education announced a "Commission on the High School Senior Year," calling the senior year a "lost opportunity that we need to reclaim." While some students try to get by with as little work as possible, others find it the most stressful year of their lives, with more demanding courses, more leadership responsibilities in their extracurricular activities, and the added burden of applying to college and taking the requisite college entrance tests.

There is often an enormous amount of tension about choosing and being admitted to the "right" college. Students and their families react to this particular stress in a number of ways, and many want the college admissions process over with as soon as possible.

Early Decision (a program in which students apply by November 1 and agree to attend if admitted in mid-December) and Early Action (adhering to the same dates but allowing students to apply to other colleges later) have become increasingly popular in recent years, partly because admitted students are thus relieved of the pressures of college admissions well before the normal spring notification date. While there are many good reasons not to apply early to college (among them the fact that the senior year often provides a great deal more information about which colleges might provide the best match), many students admitted early report they are grateful for some respite from the stresses they have experienced during high school. Some use the balance of the senior year and the summer to discover new academic and extracurricular interests and to pursue learning for its own sake, not simply for grades. They point to that period as the first "breather" they have had since early childhood.

Some high schools help all of their seniors in the transition from high school to college by allowing a slightly reduced course load, along with alternatives such as community service, research projects, and internships that might help with career exploration.

Colleges can help themselves as well as their prospective students by declaring (and demonstrating) that they are not judged simply by the number of AP or other advanced credits amassed at the end of senior year. For example, those students with particular strengths in the humanities and social sciences often believe colleges expect them to take calculus when they might be much better served by another algebra course or statistics—or another language—instead. No matter which path they take, students who can find ways to reduce stress and use the senior year well arrive at college much better prepared to take full advantage of their first year of college.

Taking Time Off Before or During College

Perhaps the best way of all to get the full benefit of a "time-off" is to postpone entrance to college for a year. For almost thirty years, Harvard has recommended this option, indeed proposing it in the letter of admission. In addition, after all the places in the current class are filled, a small number of outstanding applicants have been offered the opportunity to come to Harvard for the subsequent academic year. Normally a total of about fifty to seventy students defer college until the next year.

The results have been uniformly positive. Harvard's daily student newspaper, *The Crimson,* reported that students who had taken a year off found the experience "...so valuable that they would advise all Harvard students to consider it" (May 19, 2000). In fact, about 20 percent of Harvard students follow the practice of "time out" at some point before graduation. Harvard's overall graduation rate of 97 percent is among the highest in the nation, perhaps in part because so many students take time off. One student, noting that the majority of her friends will simply spend eight consecutive terms at Harvard, "wondered if they ever get the chance to catch their breath."

During her year off, the student quoted above toured South America with an ice-skating company and later took a trip to Russia. Another interviewed in the article worked with a growing e-commerce company (in which the staff grew from 10 to 100 during the year) and backpacked around Europe for six months.

Some Options for the Interim Year

Members of the Class of 2004 took part in the following activities, and more, in the interim year:

exploring

or living

or studying

or teaching

or training

or traveling

or working—in:

drama, figure skating, health-care, historical mines, hospitals, kibbutz life, language study, mineralogical research, missionary work, music, non-profit groups, orphanages, presidential campaigns, rebuilding schools, special needs volunteering, sports, steel drumming, storytelling, student politics, swing dance, university courses, and writing—

in the following locales:

Belize, Brazil, China, Costa Rica, Denmark, Ecuador, France, Germany, Guatemala, Honduras, India, Ireland, Israel, Italy, Mongolia, Nepal, Philippines, Scandinavia, Scotland, Spain, Switzerland, Taiwan, Thailand, Uruguay, United States, and Zimbabwe.

Many students divide their year into several segments of work, travel, or study. Not all can afford to travel or to take part in exotic activities. A number have served in the military or other national service programs. Some remain at home, working, taking part-time courses, interning, and still finding the time to read books they have never had time to fit into their schedules, or they begin to write the "great American novel." Others have been able to forge closer ties with parents or grandparents from whom they may have drifted away during the hectic pace of the high-school years.

Reactions to the Year Off

Students taking a year off prior to Harvard are doing what students from the U.K. do with their so-called "gap year." Other countries have mandatory military service for varying periods of time. Regardless of the reason why they took the year off or what they did, students could not be more effusive in their praise. Many talk of their year away as a "life-altering" experience or a "turning point," and most feel that its full value can never be measured and will pay dividends the rest of their lives. Many come to college with new vision of their academic plans, their extracurricular pursuits, the intangibles they hoped to gain in college, and the many career possibilities they observed in their year away. Virtually all would do it again.

Nevertheless, taking time off can be a daunting prospect for students and their parents. Students often want to follow friends on safer and more familiar paths. Parents worry that their sons and daughters will be sidetracked from college, and may never enroll. Both fear that taking time off can cause students to "fall behind" or lose their study skills irrevocably. That fear is rarely justified. High school counselors, college administrators, and others who work with students taking time off can help with reassurance that the benefits far outweigh the risks.

Occasionally students are admitted to Harvard or other colleges in part because they accomplished something unusual during a year off. While no one should take a year off simply to gain admission to a particular college, time away almost never makes one a less desirable candidate or less well prepared for college.

Achieving Balance

While the focus here has been on ways to relieve stress for today's high- achieving generation, we should note that in fact most students are coping well with pressure, even thriving. This is a remarkable time, with opportunities that previous generations (and students in many other countries today) could not imagine. Colleges, for example, now reach out through their recruiting programs to talented students from every economic background. Financial aid makes college a reality for outstanding students on a scale that was not possible before. Graduation rates at leading American colleges and universities remain extremely high and students express satisfaction with their college experiences.

It is important to remember that access to higher education around the world is at present limited to a lucky few. Those fortunate enough to enjoy such a privilege have a responsibility to use their talents to provide expanded opportunities for future generations. So far, most young alumni and alumnae have been successful in meeting the formidable challenges they have faced since college. But they continue to remind us that the rigors of competing in the new world economy impose high standards on everyone. They do not (nor do we) tell their peers to "slack off" and achieve less. Recent graduates advise today's high school and college students to prepare themselves emotionally as well as academically.

It is worth noting that extraordinary achievements are never based on emulating someone else's achievements, but on some unmeasurable combination of (a) marching to one's own specific and unique drummer and (b) accidentally—perhaps unconsciously—doing something that captures the Zeitgeist in new and unexpected ways. Those whom parents often want their children to emulate either used their own ingenuity to give the public a product or image it desperately wanted, or happened to catch a hot wave of the time, or (ideally) both.

While their achievement stands as an ideal for which others strive, others cannot by definition duplicate that achievement because it is induplicable. The problem can often be well-meaning but misguided parents who try to mold their children into an image of success they value; and their children, being moldable as they are, often get on board and go along with the program before they have any capacity to make such a choice for themselves. Yet the paradox is that the only road to real success is to become more fully oneself, to succeed in the field and on the terms that one oneself defines.

So the pressures placed on many children, while undoubtedly inculcating a constricting discipline in a child's life, probably have the unintended effect of delaying a child's finding him or herself and succeeding on his or her own terms. We should all have the right to gape with awe at Michael Jordan's achievements or Yo-Yo Ma's musical triumphs, while at the same time achieving our own more modest ones in our own fields and ways: finding hominid bones that shift our conception of paleontology, or composing smooth jazz melody, or tracing the rise and decline of Roman gentes. Parents and students alike could profit from redefining success as fulfillment of the student's own aims, usually yet to be discovered. Burn out is an inevitable result of trying to live up to alien goals. Time out can promote discovery of one's own passions.

The fact remains that there is something very different about growing up today. Some students and families are suffering from the frenetic pace, while others may be coping but are enjoying their lives less than they would like. Even those who are doing extraordinarily well, the "happy warriors" of today's ultra-competitive landscape, are in danger of emerging perhaps a bit less human as they try to keep up with what may be increasingly unrealistic expectations.

The good news is that students themselves offer helpful suggestions about how best to handle the challenges they face. In part because of all the obstacles that confront them from the earliest stages of their lives, this generation has emerged generally more mature, sophisticated, and, at their best, better prepared to cope with the demands of the twenty-first century. They learn at an early age how to cope with both victory and defeat and with the formidable demands placed on them by adults and peers. Yet many would benefit from a pause in their demanding lives. Let us hope that more of them will take some sort of time out before burn out becomes the hallmark of their generation.

Sanity Check

Bruce J. Poch
Vice President and Dean of Admissions, Pomona College

"It is this intrusion [of self-identified experts] that has pushed so many to forget that this process is really about education."

"The irony of the Information Age is that it has given new respectability to uninformed opinion."
John Lawton, American Broadcaster's Association

In this generation, we still have word problems about planes, trains, and automobiles heading in different directions at different speeds. The test taker is supposed to calculate arrival times, weight and height of the passengers, and maybe figure out whether or not they really give a damn about the trip anyway.

Welcome to the admissions process. Bringing different heights, weights, and speeds to the equation, the test takers, starting from different points, are hurtling to some destination in a competition that creates anxiety for the problem solvers. Like the big test, the answers are truly multiple choices and sometimes one must check the ominous "all of the above." Some guessing is okay, but do be wary of fractional points off for wrong answers.

Reflecting those elements tossed together, admission to college has become a public question; examination of the process reaches beyond the selection of colleges by a student or the construction of an entering class by the admissions office. At times, even those of us who have made our lives as members of academic communities fall to the intrusion of self-identified experts who offer their guides, their websites, their legislative remedies, and their op-ed pieces. The focus is on the process, not the education at the other side.

It is this intrusion that has pushed so many to forget that this process is really about education. This reductionism causes people to think there are only ten, or perhaps twenty, colleges and universities in the United States. It urges students, even if unintentionally, to focus on admissions not as a moment to explore a match between their interests and needs and the offerings of the institution, but, instead, to focus on the process that determines how one "gets in." Motivations about "getting in" have shifted in a way that may cause seventeen-year-olds to make difficult and, at times, uncalled for ethical choices. Long before college, students have learned to game, to try to play to a process, but they often have inadequate tools to evaluate what is before them. They strategize admission, rather than really moving to understand a college's offerings and examining their own capacities and learning styles.

So many different definitions of perfect places collide, and so much clamor about "the best" keeps students from finding their own truth. It may be worse for parents, whose investment in the admission process and concern about their notion of a right outcome may be overwhelming and even debilitating.

Information gathering and the admissions process have become complicated by these multiple and frequently contradictory interpretations. The problem isn't varied opinion, but rather, the incapacity of many entering the process to sort through the noise. Instead of taking the opinions at face value, coming from diverse sources, many are confused. Sources of 'objective information' have become incredibly suspect. Oracles of wisdom disagree publicly. Opposing voices are louder and more accusatory, enough so as to make the floor of the House of Representatives seem almost civil by comparison.

Publishers fill shelves with "how-to" books stylized by their parochial analyses of the selection process. There are interesting stories and well considered presentations. There is also an abundant supply of printed matter on the subject of college admissions which reads like the tabloids.

Consider recent articles on college admission in major newspapers across the country. Pick any recent year. Front-page stories about the admission process run in many national magazines, newspapers, and television reports. Yet, beneath those headlines, even some highly regarded publications succumb to the sensational rather than educating. There is no shortage of comment on college admission from opinion leaders in other fields, too. Dare to "google" "college admissions" and "university admissions"; my last exploration resulted in more than 460,000 hits, and that doesn't include major newspapers. Be prepared to spend hours swimming through the published material or, more importantly, develop your frame of reference and know where to look for best answers.

Colleges in general, and admissions offices in particular, love the spotlight but hate the microscope. Any process which isn't perfectly driven by numbers (even ignoring that there are hugely imperfect numbers in those formulae) looks like it operates using smoke and mirrors. The opaque quality in this cynical century translates quickly into suspicion. As selectivity increases, so does the difficulty of explaining any individual admission decision. Sadly, admissions officers haven't been good teachers about this process because the smoke and mirrors has, so far, worked to our advantage. Or, they once did. Michael Moore may be lurking.

Fundamentally, we ask, "Why is the admission process so interesting?" Is it because college admission reflects a rite of passage? Quietly we must acknowledge that it *is* at some level about the selection and creation of the next American elite. It *is* about how that opportunity pie gets sliced and about some deeply entrenched notions about who owns that pie in the first place. The Supreme Court weighed in on part of that question in June 2003. So, the answer is: "all of the above."

While consumer warning labels about counsel in the college admission process could fill a substantial volume by themselves, there is good reason to look not at what to avoid, but rather, what to jump into, head first. Families face many obstacles, not least of which is clarity and honesty in this ever more convoluted process. This essay hopes to describe some of the obstacles families face while offering some method of finding clarity along the way.

Solutions always require work, not shortcuts, and not the quick handing over of responsibility for the process to a third party. Know that. Know that this is not like buying a refrigerator or car on sale, with every detail spelled out in *Consumer Reports*. Part of the work is in creating your own method of analysis and information collection. In truth, sometimes it is best not to know too much and, sometimes, a little knowledge is dangerous.

I suggest to friends whose children are beginning this college search process that they have to invest time, intelligence, and healthy skepticism, not just look for ways to game a system which, because of the new generation of interested third parties (admissions camps, test preparation companies, college guides, even newspaper and magazine publishers), have built an elaborate system to game them.

My hope is to offer something of a framework for dealing with this college admissions lunacy or, at least, to provide a few reasons not to become crazy in the process. The most basic advice I have for you is: CALM DOWN. You will, in the end, likely thrive, not just survive.

This once was a nine-month process, at most. Sorting through the college admission process now generally seems to run about eighteen months or, in some schools and a handful of particularly nervous areas around the country, fourteen years or more. Some have allowed their thinking to become corrupted and have worked to build ways not to get their children educated well, but rather to market themselves, somehow constructed down to the bone marrow, to present well by having gone to the right schools and participated in the right programs, and to parrot the right words to admissions officers. Students have learned to become supplicants rather than applicants. They can lose their soul in the process or, in what may be even more frightening to the obsessed parent, they may lose their appeal to admissions officers at many colleges because they have homogenized and pasteurized their offspring to the point of making the child uninteresting even if their resume is fascinating.

On the other side, while admissions officers seem at times weary and increasingly cynical, it is from a hell of our own making. We look and listen to the stories each year of people for whom this is entirely new and, for some, entirely frightening. We need to remember that this is, for every applicant, a new experience. Teenage lives are supposed to have been simpler, but we all know, no matter where one lives, that has never really been true.

I present my thoughts, mindful of the fact that I was no model of clarity in my own search for the right college and, thankfully, knowing much more today from an entirely different angle. I offer here the general advice I give to friends as they enter the process with their own children. These words are delivered sometimes to heretofore-rational people strategizing and manipulating and becoming what they had derided a few years earlier.

In my own case, my mother was nagging the fall of my senior year when she asked if I had any plans to attend college and, if so, whether or not I had given any thought to writing away to get some applications. I wrote for "college bulletins," as they were called. The photos were in black and white and that wasn't a cool design element. I perused the dense handbooks (known then as a leading cause of narcolepsy) as well as *The Underground Guide to Colleges*, complete with its information about "ratio of cats to chicks." More on that gem and its successors later.

To the students, I ask, do you already feel a need for Maalox and Advil? If not, perhaps your parents do. In the end, the meeting of needs is what much of a good admissions process is all about. There are ways to figure out "best fit."

What do colleges say versus what do they do? How may that be deciphered? Colleges want socioeconomic diversity within their student bodies. High schools have worked on the latter to maintain the strength of their college acceptance lists. Colleges often want students from all over the country. But, in some areas, the parents and students have still maintained notions that college must be no more than 50 to 100 miles away. The result of that concentration is that often top kids from high performing schools make applications to a too short list of institutions. This bunching up can be self-defeating. Is a longer drive or a plane ride out of the question?

There are fundamental questions students should ask themselves:

- Are you self-disciplined or do you need to be pushed to do your work?

- Do you learn best in discussion and interactive classes or in lectures?

- How important to you is the ability to work closely with faculty and with intellectual peers?

- How much flexibility do you need, want, and can you handle in a curriculum?

- Do you *really* know with certainty what you want to do with your life? With a major?

- Is it much of an issue for you or your family that you graduate in four years?

- Does any of the above tell you anything useful?

None of these are trivial matters. They go to the heart of your educational experience. Your ability to think out loud, in an interview or an essay on these subjects, can help immensely. It is expected that your notions and thoughts on these subjects will evolve over the course of your junior and senior year in high school, just as they will during the early years of college enrollment. But, these questions are often ignored or just sublimated in favor of issues that should be trivial. Much of the advice from friends and family members pushes the cocktail party sort of analysis—a name game obsession—rather than imparting any real wisdom about colleges or what they offer.

The fundamental question remains: Whom can you trust? Is it the guidance counselors in school? (Yes, if you are lucky.) Parents—yes, but only if the information they use isn't mired in a different reality of twenty to twenty-five years ago. Friends—probably—the admissions grapevine there can be effective, especially if you know well and trust the source. How about yourself?

Many may disagree with me, but I believe you *should* work hard at this. It shouldn't be easy. It is an investment of four years of your life. It is an investment of a lot of energy, time, and someone's money.

If you read them closely, you will realize that view books and even application questions will tell you a great deal about the values and style of the college you are researching. Make the effort to do that close reading. It is your future, and no one else should prepackage your approach to the process.

What do admissions officers do when we look at colleges with our own children?

We talk to the faculty, we eavesdrop in dining halls and lounges, we not only assess the intellectual caliber of students by using statistics but we listen to the conversations, even the seemingly ridiculous and non-academic ones. How do students play intellectually? Doesn't that tell me a lot? How do they play socially? Is there a culture of collaboration or competition? How do they treat each other in a lab or seminar? Where and how do they live? And does that affect both the social and academic realms?

How about the faculty? How do they interact with each other as well as with the students? Are they really role modeling? How well do they know their colleagues, including those outside their own department or division? Is there much talk across academic departmental lines?

I urge prospective students or their parents to try to get hold of a faculty handbook to see where the teaching and research obligations are placed relative to each other. I'd look to understand the nature and expectation of faculty involvement in the governance of the institution, and (if my own institutional affiliation doesn't provide enough of a clue about my bias) I'd surely look to understand the value of teaching at that college.

I would ask as much as possible about faculty advising and work to explore just what it is that students experience, not just as juniors and seniors who have declared their major, but particularly as first and second year students. I urge a careful examination of the academic and personal advising of many different students when you visit the college. You can also use email contacts to get at that information. I do believe the focus on experience of students at those early moments in their academic career will answer substantial questions about any institution's values.

Ask where faculty live in relation to the campus and ask about their visibility in the evenings or at meal times or lectures or athletic or theater events, or just plain "after hours." Ask how students really feel about their interactions. Ask those who graduated a year or two earlier about how well supported they were in their pursuits both on and off campus. Ask about their ability to connect with faculty after graduation to later get letters of reference, since so many students now either take some pause between undergraduate and graduate education and also because students do change jobs and occupational direction more frequently.

Look at the composition of the student body, as well. Ask "who are the students?", not just "what are their scores?" "Is the social and competitive structure such that I genuinely will have the opportunity to learn things from my classmates?"

"What does the college do in its approach to teaching and learning that will allow me to fully develop critical skills? Will that approach best equip me for the job market? How flexible will my skills be?" Ask not only about class *size* but class *style*. Who does the undergraduate teaching? Who runs discussion sections, graduate students or faculty? What is the composition of the faculty in terms of degrees, departmental distribution, gender, and race? Is that important? Is the classroom style interactive or purely lecture format? Are there seminars, and at what point do they kick in, first year or senior year? Is research a possibility? Is undergraduate research at a research university really a probability or possibility? I ask these with personal biases, but surely, too, knowing that misperception is a dangerous part of this process, and confusions about what things are available to students often lead to the bitterest disappointments and may ultimately result in a transfer application. Colleges are filled with counter-intuitive possibilities.

There are obstacles to learning all of this. Colleges have been exceptionally brilliant, if unintentional, in their creation of market frenzy that so plainly and painfully has led to admission process obsession during the past twenty years. If not brilliant, we are, at least, responsible as the unindicted co-conspirators. "The obsessed" will be my shorthand for a diversity of school counselors, parents, journalists (who may also be parents and whose interests, concerns, and outright anxieties reflect their own and serve as a proxy for the rest of us), and students whose terror alert levels have increased hideously and unfortunately.

The benefactors of that anxiety have been the creators of dozens of guides and ratings instruments, the test makers, and those who have turned a cottage industry into a multibillion-dollar part of the nation's economy. (It's frequently hard to tell if these are services, let alone goods.)

The obsessed, sadly, have diverted attention from the important things students and their families ought to consider seriously when exploring colleges. Process questions, at most, should be second order issues, though clearly they have distracted many journalists, counselors, prospective students, and even the courts, as pages upon pages have been produced trying to analyze statistically and/or critically what, in selective institutions, so often is simply an intuitive process of evaluating candidacies in local institutional contexts.

Process orientation has pushed parents to make strategic choices not on the right college for the best fit for their child but on the "right college" in terms of reported reputation or prestige. Virtually every reader knows some parents who have programmed their kids from birth: the right pre-school, the right kindergarten and elementary school, and the right secondary schools, after-school activities, sports, community service, musical instrument, and summer tour and museum programs. They are the ones we laugh at in movies, the ones we shake our heads at during the PTA meeting, and who, in a moment of confession, can stare back at even the most careful of us in the mirror if we get caught in the storm.

But, here is the surprise. Most deans of admissions at the most highly selective colleges and universities in the country are of middle class or lower income origins, having attended public or parochial schools. They often didn't have available to them when they were attending school the opportunities, or even the awareness, of travel, summer experiences, private schooling, or, most especially, the sense that any of that stuff mattered. And, guess what? It's still the case that most of the students to whom even the most selective institutions offer admission come from lives which have been more modest and whose assumptions were few. In the vast majority of cases, the admitted students weren't programmed. They did what they loved, did it well, and even if rough around the edges, they did it naturally.

College admission officers, while acknowledging many options for students, have convincingly asserted that where one goes to college *is* important for a series of sometimes-intangible benefits. From promises of résumés that open doors and connect students to professional networks, we created "decal envy." The owner of the right decal in the rear window of the family car seems sometimes to declare parenting success through the accomplishments of progeny; we have been persuaded by our own rhetoric. And, in some cases, for very good reason. In other cases, well, perhaps not so much.

The forprofit side of the college admissions industry has changed in the past twenty-five years, too, straying far from the old standard bearer, sleep-inducing college guides which reported the pabulum collected from colleges in dry text while making some attempt to label institutions as "most selective" or "selective," the former, of course, being the height of prestige.

From print media to the explosion of material on the Web, families need tools with which to navigate the ever more polluted waters of information. What is available? Wander to a number of the old guard guide websites and the benefit may still be relief for insomnia. Look to instruments such as *U.S.News & World Report* and drown in data which takes the web surfer or reader only part way to discovering institutions which make sense for any student. (To be fair, the editors of *U.S.News & World Report* do warn families of the ranking limitations, though, to be critical, that print is awfully small for those of us over forty and is bypassed quickly as our limited attention spans jump to the bottom line.) Or look to The Princeton Review website which provides "counselor-o-matic," a controversial device designed to match students with colleges. Fuzzy logic does not seem to exist in this world, but the cynics as system architects do, at least in the past, through included questions such as "Has your family donated buckets of cash to a college?" While perhaps funny in some privileged worlds, it leaves students who have real financial concerns often feeling defeated before they get half way through that search and, worse, is just plain wrong in its supposition in 99.9 percent of admission cases (which Princeton Review insists is the principal point of the question, but, to my eye, where irony doesn't translate well to the web).

In the 1970s, the world of college guides started to change with the introduction of the *Yale Daily News Insider's Guide to Colleges* and *The Underground Guide to Colleges*, complete with the information about "ratio of cats to chicks," which had an even more profound effect, though it is now defunct. Students considered *The*

Underground Guide a definitive guide for those wanting an insider's look at college life, activity, and social possibilities. The language for that time was graphic and, therefore, very cool. (Today, its language would read almost like *Newsweek*.) It explicitly described the climate for things such as alcohol and drugs, and sexual behavior and permissiveness on a campus-by-campus basis. That, of course, was before Lisa Birnbach's *The Preppie's Guide to Colleges* that was a sanitized, if smug, Reagan-era guide. As far as I could tell, it was remarkably fictional in many college descriptions. Today's version, *The Princeton Review's Best 351 Colleges* (the number of colleges included may change), though much more thorough in its data collection, still seems an odd hybrid of the Birnbach and Underground guides. It is playful, and sometimes quite on-target. It is also quite edgy and therefore entertaining. Occasionally the editors are seduced by the need to be snide at the expense of providing a big or even accurate picture.

The dinosaur in any college admission conversation is The College Board, a membership organization often vilified for its famous standard-bearer, the SAT. It, too, has mutated, sometimes oddly, as its own ventures spread to test prep materials, guide books, statistical and research services for colleges and universities, and its own marketing forces for those services. They currently use the vocabulary of customer relations and marketing once considered taboo in higher education. The College Board, while providing some of the most substantial and valuable information, meetings, and colloquia for member institutions and essential research to many other organizations, including the courts, also behaves frequently in a confused manner, not quite knowing if it is a membership organization or a marketing force. No wonder students, parents, educators, and even their own members get confused in dealing with them.

The proliferation of guidebooks continues, and they are filled with statistics and build on the supposition that numbers equal truth. Numbers, of course, in the American experience, mark things as "valid." Guides rank institutions in their respective peer categories while creating artificial precision and translating that into enormous marketing success. The reader relies upon someone else's system to determine weights and balances of what is good and important. We lazily and easily forgive what they may exclude, even if one or more institutions we seem interested in may have built their college on that thing relegated to the sidelines.

Intuition alone should tell a rational person that things get ranked to reflect the publisher's choices of priorities and weights. If comparing general education programs or a mix in a student body is what is truly important to a student or their family, they will be disappointed to find consideration of those values noticeably absent from most guides. Too few readers look beyond the gross rankings, let alone the weights assigned to the individual parts or to tables which in those guides may reveal separations in rank created by a tenth of a point on a particular scale.

It is the American bent toward ranking and absolutes that creates this artificial precision and apparent need to fit something complicated into a neat, newsbyte–sized package. It leads us to manufacture ratings and rankings for some things that can't be fully quantified. We are left with numbers that reveal nothing more than a distinction without a difference. Or, worse, we are left with real distinctions entirely masked because of the limited analytic view, spurred more by advertising rates and sales volume than by any truly solid attempts to discern subtle or substantively different intention of program or mix in a student body or faculty.

One guidebook several years ago was simply called *"Guide to the Right Colleges."* The title, though playful, meant the political "right" and offered several hundred pages slamming institutions with any "liberal" bent in the curriculum or vague whiff of it in the student body. That was perfectly reasonable for some consumers, but for others was entirely off-base. In short, be thoughtful while perusing guidebooks. They have editorial viewpoints, meaning there can sometimes be a problem of relative truth, too. "Fair and balanced" can't be trademarked and can have multiple meanings in today's world. Just ask Fox News.

If it is not enough to crunch numbers furiously, there are the famous "reputational surveys" which are converted into a point system with disturbing frequency. In the *U.S.News & World Report* version these often reflect professional associations, friendships, and familiarity because of geographic proximity of presidents and deans, rather than substantive thinking or rigorous analysis. I get to vote for whom I like or know or for the institutions they represent. Or against those I don't like. Yet, most college presidents and admissions deans and deans of faculty have complied or bought-in. We play the game. Our trustees like our colleges to be high on the lists. We vote.

Can rankings lead to real changes and improvements, or do guides merely report trends? Some universities already have set out to change the way they teach or to structure class size in a way to benefit rankings, which may yield some very good effects educationally. Real attention to the undergraduate student in some institutions where such students were forsaken at the altar of research seems to have reemerged recently, but the threat to the genuine integrity of an academic program, suddenly reinvented to accommodate a best-selling guide, is troublesome, at the least. It should push a parent or prospective student to ask about the nature of academic planning at that institution and to ask about real values that underpin the curriculum. Of course, the rules of the game may shift from year to year and the weighted components of a ranking may ultimately punish the school that sought a particular rankings reward by gaming.

The Princeton Review website includes discussion message boards in which sixteen- and seventeen-year-olds advise and counsel each other about "best" and "worst" and how to write an essay or what rumor is afloat about any given institution. From a sociological standpoint, it is a fascinating but sometimes horrifying glimpse into the panic, rumor mongering, and college-obsessed minds of the authors, but it also is gasoline added to an already enormous fire of confusions. (And, they talk a lot about sex and drugs. *The Underground Guide* still breathes!) Much of the chatter on that site is just plain wrong, and many if not all of the questions could be answered simply by a call to the college in question or even a passing glance at that institution's view book. Taking peer counsel as sage wisdom boggles the mind, but it clearly signals complete distrust of answers from the colleges and their representatives. That is a tragic state of affairs and something we in college admissions offices must recognize and work to remedy.

Worse is the "parents only" message board on that same website, where those whose powers of discernment should be better honed add to the chat, and the parents reveal themselves too frequently, if unintentionally, as frightened—and sometimes quite clearly as manipulative—schemers living through their children at the expense of rationality and real support for their sons and daughters. It reads like a therapy group that could be called *Admissions Anonymous.* But, alas, there is no therapist, just undisciplined, unmoderated chatter. A look at the timestamps on the messages reveals a lot. The postings come in at all hours of the night, reflecting a sleep-deprived state. The dangerous advice found in the student section is hugely amplified in the "parents only" section, where there is even greater presumed authoritative information. Yikes.

A very popular guide/book/website uses what political fundraisers call "push polling," soliciting current students at several hundred colleges and universities who were already visiting the site to answer survey questions in lieu of on-site visits that were formerly made to write the guides. It is interesting to consider just which students, after enrolling in college, would routinely go back to the college guide site. What remains unrevealed in the guide is some real statistical reporting about how many current students answered each question on the survey and what that may or may not adequately represent. This is not scientific polling. To their credit, editors of some guides have provided advance copy to colleges under review so that gross errors may be vetted and embarrassment on both sides avoided.

Those in the college search process face odd corporate relationships, too. One of the standard-bearer guides, *Petersons,* solicits data and asks colleges to participate in some free distribution of the "guide to selective colleges" issue by sponsoring the lists. They charge for the self-descriptions. Is this a guide or an advertising directory? That company recently acquired a web-based college essay editing company, whose services they market and which, sadly, has left open very serious questions of ethics, conflict of interest, and the fundamental question of authorship of essays. In a number of reported cases, the same packaged and therefore plagiarized essay from that firm appeared over the signature of multiple candidates in college applicant pools. A few landed on my desk. Many plagiarists were discovered, resulting in immediate rejection of their applications. Was the website an "enabler?"

Another company has successfully and nationally made arrangements with high schools to survey students in class. The lists are supposed to generate scholarship opportunities, and, in many cases, they do result in student names being purchased by colleges and announcing financial support possibilities. The lists, according to a *Wall Street Journal* article, also are resold to anything from banks to furniture companies.

Know that reporting and statistical analysis can be predicated upon fiction even when the intention is to present solid fact. (Remember the confusions that still exist between "data" and "fact.") *U.S.News & World Report* relies upon honest answers to its survey and it was stunning to learn that some colleges got caught when their reported data was, well...exaggerated. Or, to parse the language, the questions were interpreted somewhat differently than one in the mainstream reasonably could have assumed. One amazing example was the college that answered the question about the percentage of living alumni who donated to the annual fund with a carefully crafted subset. Those who had not donated within five years were considered "dead" by the development office: not just dead-beats but DEAD! (There is a nice convenient way to change a denominator for a better result!!!)

Some websites ask for students to rate colleges, sometimes presuming that the rater is a current student. It's too easy for college rivalries or pranks to play out in these sites, which have little if any verification of the source. Yet, with peculiar comfort, so many take anything on the web to be true, without examining sources, that these instruments frequently thrive, regardless of their real worth. John Lawton of the American Broadcasters' Association said, in 1995, "The irony of the Information Age is that it has given new respectability to uninformed opinion."

It would be easy to focus only on the gaming from the college side of the equation. Some play the statistics game in interesting ways and it's been eye-opening for even those of us who have been around for a long time to discover the different definitions that lead to calling something an "application." Sounds odd, but it does then determine the question, "How many applied? What percentages were offered admission? Funny, too, are the different definitions of who was "offered admission." What of early decision machinations?

What can be said of "merit" scholarships? Do the students who accept those offers get what they expected in an institution, or was the "bargain" paramount? In the end, do they have intellectual peers or the access to faculty they sought? Do they graduate in equal or larger proportions to other students at that institution? Or do they transfer away? Does the merit scholarship really go to the meritorious? In many cases, it is a discount for those with little or no financial need who will bring more tuition dollars to a college. It may leave less financial support for the bright but financially needy students. I understand why an individual would take that offer, but I cringe at the public policy implications for our future. What does that say of choices and values? There is no right answer here (but I do have an opinion).

Colleges have responsibility for much of the hype that has led to anxiety of all sorts about the admissions process. Some admissions professionals have promoted institutions with little regard to reality. Some boards of trustees and the guides they read will tell admissions officers they must reject more and more candidates to somehow establish institutional credibility by having a highly selective admission process. In the background, treasurers and trustees do notice that financial strength, measured in bond ratings evaluations—a financial instrument—now includes review of admissions selectivity and SAT scores as a part of the ultimate rating issued by Moody's Investor Services and Standard and Poor's.

As a group, colleges often hype selectivity and, at the same time, push to expand applicant pools. Each year it seems more students are applying to a smaller group of colleges, and to a larger number of schools within that select group. At highly selective institutions, students average nine to ten applications each rather than the four or five of a generation ago. Admission staffs travel farther, talk to more people, and invite more of you to our open houses to encourage your interest further and to provide you with as much information as possible in the shortest amount of time. We hope that the life preparation gained from this experience isn't just better training to survive car dealers. While within that work is a genuine effort to diversify in many ways the student body, a good proportion of the outreach still turns to those populations extremely well represented already.

Web and CD/DVD versions of college guides have been created by several companies and placed in schools. One can file applications electronically. College viewbooks moved from black and white to color in the early 90s and, some, I dare say, have moved from fact to fiction. In those beautiful books, everyone looks happy. Every college and university has outdoor classes. (If there is one bit with which I can agree from the Princeton Review, it is their observation that 95 percent of all outdoor classes are found only in viewbooks—especially when one notes the geographic location of some of those colleges.) Everyone in the books has perfect teeth and blemish free skin. No one has bad hair. Of course, then, neither will you if you choose that college.

For many students, there has been (and frankly speaking, there *should* be) some struggle to define what you *want* and what you *need* in a college. Questioning how one learns best, and under what conditions, should be the central issue in mind.

Students should find a way to ask themselves direct questions. Questions may include those about who it is that they seek as peers. In looking at each college, students should translate the description of a diverse student body into what that may mean on a given campus at a given moment. Explore the substance and thinking behind a general education program (requirements) a college offers or, if they have none, why not and what does that mean? The sorting out is to learn your own needs and to come to understand and reflect upon your own learning styles. Which classes satisfy general education requirements? How thoughtful was their inclusion of classes in the roster of general education courses? Should early decision be used for strategic purposes? Should financial aid discussions turn into something like haggling in a market place? What do students talk about? What courses are required? Is the food good? Or, might it really, in the end, be more meaningful to know on an intimate level the ways in which teaching and advising are respected and encouraged or whether the campus climate is one that remains energized over a weekend or a semester?

Sorting through all of these questions about colleges and about yourself can be daunting. The good news is that you improve your chances while improving your understanding. Students who know what they are looking for have better luck finding it and can do a better job of articulating their hopes and interests in their applications.

Visit the campus before you apply, if possible. Interview if one is offered. And, unless you are socially inept (and your counselor has the courage to tell you), plan to have an interview on campus or at least with an alum. They rarely hurt.

Know what you are talking about in the interview. No bovine residues and don't go overboard. If you have a student interviewer, do not assume this is a best friend and tell things you wouldn't tell your parents, but do take full advantage of that moment to find out as much as you are able about that person's experience and the experiences he or she can share about friends.

Listen up and listen well. Ask the same question of many people and enjoy the very different answers you will receive. That partly defines any place. And remember to have some fun with this. You can learn a lot about yourself and a lot about your family as you identify the things that really matter to each of you in this selection process. It is a two-way street. And, remember to breathe.

Editor's Stories I

Seventy-four percent of colleges surveyed by The National Association for College Admission Counseling reported undergoing an image overhaul during the 2002 - 2003 academic year.

Twenty-six percent of those colleges surveyed in the same year reported an increase in unethical admission practices.

Seattle, 1988.   Earnest Boyer, then President of The Carnegie Foundation, delivers the keynote address during a national conference of The College Board. His talk conveys concerns about the diminishing role of ethics in college admissions; his message is convincingly filled with the wisdom and joy of a life committed to education; his purpose is to inspire similar leadership in the college admissions profession. Winding his way up to a fitting conclusion, Dr. Boyer reads from the help wanted section of *The Chronicle of Higher Education*: "Admissions officer wanted," he begins, "must be articulate, engaging, savvy, and have the ability to close." Pausing purposefully, he delivers a cautionary and prophetic blow, "I am afraid we may be losing our civility faster than we are losing our students."

If Dr. Boyer were alive today, he would certainly be astonished by the proliferation of admission practices he cautioned against— practices he would probably characterize as educationally unethical; practices driven by marketing—a concept just beginning to be discussed among admission professionals in 1988.

The 1980s had presented colleges with a unique and ominous combination of challenges: a forecast of decreasing numbers of seventeen-year-olds, less government support for colleges and for student financial aid, and rising operational costs. College presidents, unaccustomed to being involved with admissions, suddenly became anxiously interested. "How are we going to attract enough students to stay in 'business'?" became the major concern, directing these presidents to view students as customers, to consider the management of enrollment as a business function of education, and to look to the private sector for promising marketing tools.

Today few colleges have been able to resist the pervasive influence of commercial admission practices. New language communicates and describes college admissions; new strategic thinking directs admission activities; new business savvy enrollment managers take over for admission directors to deliver and implement strategic plans—even the composition of boards of trustees and the qualifications of college presidents have all been shaped to favor business acumen. From hugely increased budgets for admissions, public relations, landscaping, upgrading dorms, and student health clubs to the hiring of external marketing specialists, commercialism has demonstrated its hold on the management of America's colleges.

Success measured by an increase in applications improves a college's market position and rank. So, many colleges have gone to extraordinary lengths to increase applications. Tactics have included: offering scholarship money to early applicants, waiving college application fees, encouraging students to apply even though they were clearly inadmissible, falsification of data, and aggressive and blatant overselling of programs and majors. While these tactics have contributed to application increases at many colleges, with disproportionate increases occurring at the most popular colleges, this success has resulted in additional controversial practices.

Yield, the percentage of admitted students who say yes to a college's admission offer, is also a measure of success. During 2002 - 2003, admission deans at the most popular colleges knew that the increase in applications meant that there were bound to be many overlaps—students with applications to many colleges—making it extremely difficult to assess the interest level of each applicant and to determine how many students to admit. Anticipating this uncertainty, colleges increased the number of students admitted under binding early decision (ED) programs to record levels. (By applying ED, students commit to attend the college, if admitted, ensuring the college an almost 100 percent yield on ED applicants and radically increasing yield statistics for the overall applicant pool.) In 2002, several of the Ivies admitted more than 40 percent of their students through Early Decision programs. This represented 5-year increases of 80 to 110 percent in ED admits for the colleges.

Another method for increasing apparent selectivity while ensuring a full fall class has been the use of waiting lists. Placing admissible students on a waiting list allows the college to admit fewer students, thereby effecting higher yield. The college can then go to its waiting list in the summer to fill any vacancies. The ranksters have no way of controlling or reporting this yield-influencing strategy, or to control enrollment amid the increasing use of multiple applications by students. The 2002 - 2003 year was indeed a "record year" for the use of lengthy waiting lists: some colleges' waiting lists exceeded the number of students initially offered admission. However, this record is certainly not touted by colleges.

Even *The Wall Street Journal* investigated and wrote about how "Colleges Spurn Best Applicants to Increase Yield and Appease US News," a summer 2002 article about how colleges have begun balancing a student's desirability with the likelihood of winning that student among competing colleges. "Since a college's rank is affected by yield, many colleges are denying the most qualified students in favor of the most likely to say yes to an offer of admission."

Additional practices that seemed counterintuitive to prevailing educational norms were reported to have increased during this year of heightened competition. A survey conducted by The National Association for College Admission Counseling reported a rise in the importance of cumulative GPA (up 18 percent) relative to the importance of college prep curriculum GPA (down 8 percent) when selecting students. This shift contradicted common professional beliefs that college prep curriculum GPA is a better predictor of college success because it represents work in tougher courses. Knowing this, and that cumulative GPAs are almost always higher, it seems that some admission officials decided to favor cumulative GPAs solely for their positive impact on the college's rank.

The groundswell of interest in managing image by improving rank has also resulted in giving more weight to SAT scores when admitting students, since a college's average SAT scores are given significant consideration in determining its rank. This practice is accelerating despite increasingly prominent evidence about the educational shortcomings of the SAT, including a spring 2002 *Boston Globe* article describing how coaching for the SAT helps those who can afford it take advantage of admissions and scholarship opportunities: "The real winners with the SAT are The College Board and the test prep industry." The colleges' increasing use of the SAT and The College Board's silence about that use raise concerns about the exercise of educational authority in college admissions.

Finally, the use of merit scholarships to influence rank by luring academic stars has accelerated with intense ferocity. Some colleges offer to beat any other college's scholarship offer; some vendors promise to get the best financial packages for their student clients. This often instigates bidding wars among colleges for students whose parents or agents are shrewd enough to call financial aid officers and mention the competition's offer. "I have the files of five students on my desk," complained an admission dean during a recent phone conversation. "All of the parents are lying about the competing offers they are receiving from other colleges. I feel like a car salesman. It has got to stop."

Our Numbers Are Up! (Is That Good?)

Mark Speyer
Director of College Counseling, Columbia Grammar &
Preparatory School

"We are torturing our young people, and sending them less prepared to college than they were ten years ago."

1. The Soviet plant manager and the manipulable numbers.

My first economics class in the early sixties taught about the misallocations of resources characteristic of a Soviet-style planned economy. If the manager of a Soviet book production plant were judged by the number of books produced, we learned, inevitably the books would grow shorter and smaller, until there were indeed lots of books, but each with very few pages. If the manager were judged by the number of pages, inevitably there would be fewer and fewer words per page, until there were lots of pages with very little on them. If judged by the number of words, the manager would see to it that books become wordier and wordier, to the point of unreadability. In short, whatever number was used to evaluate the plant manager would increase dramatically, given the manager's obvious incentives and powers to increase it.

2. Manipulable college numbers are up: the number of applicants and the SAT average.

I think of that plant manager every time another gleeful college representative tells me that "Our numbers are up." The numbers in question, of course, are not the number of books in the library, or the number of tenured professors who teach undergraduates, or the number of dollars available for financial aid, or the number of students participating in team and club sports, or the number participating in charitable activities, or any other number representing a change in substance. No, the numbers in question are the numbers most subject to manipulation by the admissions office: first, the total number of applicants to the college, and second, the average SAT scores of the admitted students.

3. How colleges increase the size of their applicant pools.

The total number of applicants may increase for purely external reasons, of course: more students graduating from high school, more students reading good things about a particular college. But from where I sit, the number is increasing also because admissions offices are driving it up by fair means (visiting more high schools) and foul (encouraging applicants who have no chance of admission, finding new ways to define and count "applicants").[1]

4. How colleges increase their SAT averages.

Similarly, SAT scores may be going up because American young people are simply getting smarter, reading more books, broadening their vocabularies, grasping the point of arguments faster and more effectively. But from my perspective, based on eighteen years of college counseling in Manhattan, it is more plausible that SAT scores are going up, first, because college admissions make them a more important factor every year, privileging the applicants with big numbers and playing really rough with anyone whose scores are low, and second, because high school students, in response to this trend, are spending more and more hours and more and more dollars trying to drive up their scores.

5. Bigger pools mean shorter reads, more use of numbers, more games.

The drive for a bigger applicant pool and the greater emphasis on SATs are not independent of each other. As colleges generate ever more applications, without hiring a bigger staff to read them, they necessarily rely more and more on numerical factors like the SAT, with less and less emphasis on reading and discussing essays or on evaluating a student's unusual talents. Furthermore, as they worry about how many of these applicants will actually want to enroll, they are more and more tempted to use early decision and early action programs to protect their yield, and in fact, more and more are tempted to play games of every kind, such as wait-listing super-qualified applicants they consider unlikely to attend. I believe that super-sized applicant pools are inexorably producing sillier and shallower admissions decisions. Jacques Steinberg's fine recent book on admissions at Wesleyan, *The Gatekeepers*, shows in an early chapter how hard the Wesleyan representative works to generate as many applications as possible, without worrying about whether the applicants have any chance of admission; the later chapter in which he actually reads the applications is entitled "Read Faster, Say No."[2] An officer in an Ivy League admissions office, seeking to explain a decision that made no sense to either of us, told me that this year they had just not had the staff to give all applications the time and attention they deserved. Bill Fitzsimmons of Harvard, in announcing Harvard's new policy in the spring of 2003 on early applications, said that one reason for the change was the worry that ever-increasing applicant pools threatened their ability to spend the time they needed to discuss applications in the detail needed.

6. Does it matter?

Does it matter? Name-brand colleges, some might say, have always been hard to get into; so what if they have become a lot more numbers-oriented in recent years? When the admissions game changes, ambitious students find ways to adapt to the changes, and in any case, there are lots of less selective colleges for them to go to if the more select ones don't take them.

7. Yes, it matters: it's bad for students and it's bad for education.

Well, as a college counselor, as a teacher, and not least, as a parent of teenagers, I believe it does matter. I believe that the new obsession with numbers is counter-educational: that it makes for a less educated and less educable kind of student; a less thoughtful, more cynical, more boring, and more exhausted kind of student, not at all the kind of student that colleges on a clear day know they want and need. Pumped-up SATs do *not* mean better students. Andrew Delbanco, a professor at Columbia, was a refreshing voice of skepticism and sanity in a *New York Times* Op Ed column of March 16, 2001: "Every year I read that our incoming students have better grades and better SAT scores than in the past. But in the classroom, I do not find a commensurate increase in the number of students who are intellectually curious, adventurous or imbued with fruitful doubt. Many students are chronically stressed, grade-obsessed and, for fear of jeopardizing their ambitions, reluctant to explore subjects in which they doubt their proficiency."

8. *U.S.News & World Report* and ETS into the Leadership Gap.

It is commonplace to say that the new emphasis on numbers results from the ever-growing power of the *U.S.News & World Report* rankings of colleges, and no doubt that is true. The much larger cause of the problem, however, is the lack of a clear definition in this country of what constitutes a good pre-college education. As a nation, the United States, for various historical and political reasons, has been unwilling to adopt the kind of state-developed school curricula and state-administered university entrance examinations that France has in its Baccalaureate, Germany in its Abitur, and the United Kingdom in its A-Levels. In America, the definition of what constitutes a good preparation for college is literally a free-for-all: colleges, high schools, journalists, religious leaders, politicians, parents, students—we can all put in our two cents. Still, I believe that the group most influential today in defining curricula and standards for America is our selective colleges and universities: their admissions offices, their faculties, their presidents, and provosts. But I also believe that these people carry their authority very lightly, and that they have been willing, to a shocking degree, to defer to the rankings developed by *U.S.News* and to the tests developed by ETS. President Richard Atkinson of the University of California system demonstrated pretty dramatically the power that colleges have over ETS when they choose to exercise it, but leadership like his has been sadly lacking in America, and most of his colleagues seem hopelessly addicted to the kind of numbers-are-up boasting that shows what a splendid job they are doing.

9. WHAT IS TO BE DONE?

What is to be done? I know there are many people out there smarter and wiser than I, and I hope there are organizations out there with a lot more collective knowledge and wisdom than I possess, who have better ideas than mine about how to fix the numbers problem. Still, having come this far in such a negative vein, I believe I should make a few suggestions about how to make things better.

10. Recognize the problem.

First, we must recognize that we have a problem, and stop pretending that increasing numbers mean that everything is peachy.

11. Take responsibility.

Second, we must take responsibility, individually and collectively, for the problem. It is a fundamental principle of ethics and of law that people are responsible for the predictable consequences of their actions. By this principle, every admissions rep who increases the importance of the SAT as an admissions factor is responsible for the lost time and the lost education of the students who must now spend more time prepping for the test. Every counselor, every teacher, every parent who sees the problem and doesn't protest is responsible too. "At work, I lament these developments," says Andrew Delbanco of Columbia, "but at home, I give in to them. I do not forbid my daughter, now a high school junior, from seeking help to raise her test scores." But Delbanco wrote his hard-hitting Op Ed piece for *The New York Times*, so he deserves to be considered more a part of the solution than of the problem. Every college president or admissions rep who believes that The *U.S.News* rankings are harmful, but who nonetheless advertises the high position that his or her institution has won in those rankings, is responsible for their ever-growing power. Some in small ways, some in large: as individuals, as members of organizations, as employees of institutions, we are all responsible.

12. Colleges must recognize that they define educational standards.

Third, as a very specific application of the point about taking responsibility, colleges and universities should recognize the central role they play in defining curricula and standards for secondary education in America, and should work to develop and promulgate more intelligent standards than the ones we now have. The power our federal and state governments exercise over the education of our best young people is nothing like the power that Harvard and Yale and Stanford exercise. Needless to say, our elected representative bodies have the power to define educational standards if we want them to, but so far we do not really want them to, and so the name-brand colleges must recognize that they are running the show, and running the lives of their own and of other people's children.

13a. Separate The College Board from the SAT.

Fourth, we who work in college admissions need to empower our professional organizations to address the problem. In its origin, and in theory even today, The College Board is an association of secondary schools and colleges meeting to define the procedures and standards for college admission. In its most important aspect today, however, The College Board is the company that owns the SAT and that works to defend it and to maximize its revenue. Personally, I believe The College Board cannot be true to its purpose as long as it owns the SAT, and that for its soul's sake it should give it up. The College Board should give or sell or barter the SAT to the Educational Testing Service, sever all legal and geographical connections, and then sit down and have a real, unbiased discussion about what kinds of tests and what kinds of admissions procedures will produce the best college students for our nation.

13b. Empower NACAC—The National Association for College Admission Counseling.

Similarly, we need to build NACAC into the kind of organization that can really set standards and enforce them. Yale's president and admissions office deserve credit for their leadership in criticizing and curbing the growth of early decision programs, but they deserve blame for threatening to operate outside NACAC guidelines for early programs. As President Kennedy said about the UN, NACAC is our last, best hope. With early programs we are caught in a Catch-22 situation. Individual admissions deans and directors like Fitzsimmons of Harvard say publicly they would love to end such programs, but not until their competitors end them too; yet if all the competitors get together and end them collectively, they fear that the federal government would get them for collusion. So they can't act individually, and they can't act collectively. Only an organization like NACAC can bring us out of a mess like that, and it is up to all of us to support NACAC as much as we can in the attempt.

14. Develop professional rankings.

Fifth, we should try to redeem the rankings. If colleges and universities are unhappy with the job that *U.S.News* is doing, they should set about devising and publishing their own rankings. If you want something done right, sometimes you have to do it yourself. No doubt college-based rankings would be complicated and controversial; still, peer review is a central principle of scholarship in American colleges. In every discipline there are methods and standards by which new knowledge is evaluated, and we do not believe that all assertions and all opinions are equally worthwhile. Evaluation is a central responsibility of all educational institutions, and it is the main thing college admissions offices do in the wintertime. There is no reason why colleges cannot learn to evaluate each other in the same way that they now evaluate students. Or again, perhaps NACAC or my newly independent College Board should develop the rankings. In any case, the consumers of our ridiculously expensive higher education system clearly want rankings, and until an appropriate professional body provides them, the power of the *U.S. News* rankings will only increase.

15. Confront the SAT.

Sixth, we should try to redeem—or replace—the SAT. Whenever I complain to college people about the ridiculous emphasis placed on the SAT, they tell me of their sincere belief that "there is a role for the SAT in admissions decisions." Perhaps there is, but not the role that it has taken on lately: as the most important single element in selective admissions, the most important single thing for teenagers to work on if they want to go to a super-competitive college. A very simple and sensible first step, which of course a few colleges have already taken, is to accept SAT IIs in place of SAT Is—three SAT IIs for colleges that require only the SAT I, five or more SAT IIs for colleges that have hitherto asked for the SAT I and three SAT IIs. That way, all these young people trooping off to their tutors and their prep courses would at least be learning about American history, or Latin verbs, or chemical valences—things worth knowing about in college and in life.

16. To solve a problem, first recognize that you have one.

As I said earlier, other people will have other and better solutions to the problem. The main point of this article is simply that we *do* have a problem on our hands. In spite of the increased numbers, things are *not* better than ever. We are torturing our young people, and sending them less prepared to college than they were ten years ago. All of us, college people and high school people, testmakers and teachers, college reps and high school counselors, parents and students—all of us can do a much better job than we are currently doing.

1 See Rachel Toor, *Admissions Confidential: An Insider's Account of the Elite College Selection Process* (New York: St. Martin's, 2001), page 27, on admissions at Duke: "The reason we do recruiting is to get the BWRKs [bright well-rounded kids] to apply so that we can deny them and bolster our selectivity rating. We do not say this."

2 See Jacques Steinberg, *The Gatekeepers: Inside the Admissions Process of a Premier College* (New York: Penguin Putnam, 2002), page 5: "You realize that, further down the line, a lot of these kids will end up applying and being denied," Ralph [the representative] said later. "But you can't really think about that at this stage." "Read Faster, Say No" is the title of Chapter 5; it is also the mantra of

the Wesleyan representative's wife, trying to help keep him from falling behind in his reading.

Reprinted with permission. Copyright 2004 National Association for College Admission Counseling.

Faked Figures Make Fools of Us

James M. Sumner
Dean of Admission and Financial Aid, Grinnell College

"What I wish for is the abandonment of blatant falsification of data."

At the risk of sounding pious, self-serving, and sanctimonious, can I please call for an upgrade in the accuracy of the information colleges and universities submit to various publishers about their institutions? Now, I have not walked in the shoes of those who submit badly flawed and self-defined data each year, and I may not fully appreciate the pressures they face (as Atticus Finch advised his daughter Scout in *To Kill a Mockingbird*, "You never really understand a person until you consider things from his point of view, until you climb inside his skin and walk around in it"), but the vast inaccuracy of that data leads prospective students, their families, and school counselors/ advisors far astray each year. The pressures to move up in the rankings, especially in *U.S.News & World Report*, and to build a strong class profile are great. I can't help but recall two separate years in two separate corners of the U.S. in the 1990s; in one year the admission deans/directors at Whitman, Lewis and Clark, and Pacific Lutheran in the Pacific Northwest were firmly encouraged from their offices. In another year the same thing happened at Hamilton, Colgate, and Columbia in the Northeast. All were successful, experienced, and respected educators. So, make no mistake about the vulnerability of sitting admission deans (and no institutional researcher, the other campus administrator most often charged with data submission, ever lost her/his job because of a diminished ranking or class profile). The skilled reporting of *The Wall Street Journal* pointed out some of these discrepancies a few years ago by comparing data submitted by colleges to *U.S.News & World Report* with that submitted to the major bond rating agencies. Why the differences? Submitting false data to the bond raters carries stiff legal penalties, while submitting false data to *U.S.News & World*

Report, despite their increasingly specific guidelines for data submission, carries no penalties or even double-checking.

There is often tension between admission and institutional research offices, as well as others on campus, about the interpretation of data to be submitted and the definitions guiding the process (one of my on-campus, non-admission colleagues recently observed that, "The College seems to be paying a high price so that our institutional researcher can sleep well at night"). The dynamic tension between campus offices and personnel is healthy and is not my bone of contention as I call for increased accuracy. What I wish for is abandonment of the blatant falsification of data as represented in the following examples shared with me in recent years by admission deans and other admission administrators at excellent U.S. colleges with selective admission policies (but maybe not as selective as the published data would suggest, it seems).

1. Submitting class profile data that excludes "development cases." A bit of inquiry revealed that this college excluded 20 percent of its entering class from its published profile because these students were admitted in part because of their family's financial gifts to the college, both past and anticipated. This 20 percent turned out to be the academically poorest 20 percent of the class, a group generally not otherwise admissible.

2. Publishing a class profile that excludes new students of color. The reasons here are great institutional pressures to enroll more students of color coupled with generally lower pre-college, standardized test scores (SAT and ACT).

3. Excluding recruited student athletes from the class profile. The reasons here are predictable: strong community desire for great athletic teams (from, for example, alumni, townspeople, the president, and coaches) and enrollment of athletes whose secondary school grades and ACT/SAT scores lower the class means and medians.

4. Excluding from the distributed class profile, modestly prepared new students who come to the campus for a one- to two-week pre-semester, academic catch-up program. The

notion here is that since these students arrive before the bulk of the entering class, they are described as on-going students, and, therefore, not really new students.

5. Excluding local and legacy enrollees for similar reasons. All of these exclusions must be seen in the light of severe pressures to enroll a full, academically stellar (superior scores and grades), ethnically diverse, athletic, alumni-connected, and net revenue producing class of new students.

6. Listing the total number of applications for admission as "actionable applications," regardless of the level of their completeness. The idea here is to drive up the reported number of applications and thereby drive down the percent of admitted students, resulting in the appearance of enhanced selectivity. The most common rationale for this seemingly widespread practice is to deny admission to all incomplete applications at some point late in the admission cycle, thereby making them "actionable." So, if one college reports actionable applications as only those that are truly complete, and another college uses the practice described here, the second college falsely appears to be more selective. This practice can be amplified by those colleges that use a Part I Application for Admission, often a document that is little more than an admission inquiry (requiring no fee, no essay, etc.).

7. Developing an institution's own statistical system for calculating SAT and ACT scores and then publishing those institutionally normed averages. For example, a college might determine over time via its own institutional research that their students entering with a combined SAT of 950 earn a 3.4 grade point average as a group. The college might then determine that 3.4 students as a whole (maybe using state or national data) score a predictive combined SAT score of 1110. Next, the college concludes that because grading is tougher at their school, students who score 950 should really have scored 1110. Finally, the college coverts all of its new 950 first-year students to 1110 students and reports the later figure externally.

8. Excluding enrolled students who are admitted from the waiting list. Regardless of institutional reasoning, the why seems clear: wait list admits are by definition marginal applicants within the applicant pool of any given college. A related wrinkle to this practice is that even some schools that tout their need-blind admission practice abandon that commitment as they go to their wait list.

So, if we assume what has been shared with me, and passed along to you here, is more or less accurate, what can be done to better serve the college, consuming public, prospective students, their parents, and their school advisors? As a start, here are three simple suggestions:

1. Agree to a better set of firmly adhered to definitions that govern the reporting of admission data. Both the Higher Education Data Sharing Consortium (HEDS) and the Integrated Postsecondary Education Data System (IPEDS) have made progress in this regard, but more is needed. Maybe the definitions used by the bond rating corporations have something to offer. Or maybe the National Association for College Admission Counseling (NACAC) should broker a set of standard definitions followed by a set of penalties aimed at member violators.

2. Return to the traditional admission advising philosophy of helping each prospective student with whom we come in contact find the best college "match." This would require a top-down emphasis on each campus that the admission staff seek the student that is the best "fit" for that college. Trustees and presidents are seldom focused on this approach, and at the same time they fret about student retention; if the goal were to encourage the promotion to and selection of the best institutionally suited students, not only would the consuming public be better served, but student retention would increase as well.

3. Print, publish, and submit more than one entering class profile. Maybe one good way to inform prospective students is to create an overall class profile (all enrollees), and then sub-set profiles for student athletes, legacies (i.e., chips), wait list

admittees, students of color, and locals. In each case the number of students in the category would be listed and each prospective applicant for admission could clearly see where she might fit into the enrolling group. To do the same thing for all admitted (as opposed to enrolled) students would cast further light on an all too cloudy dataset.

Admissions Messages vs. Admissions Realities

Paul Marthers
Dean of Admission, Reed College

> *"If all you want is a good education (and you want that more than you want a name-brand degree), you can get a good education just about anywhere."*

Some students enter the college application process by choice; they send colleges letters or emails, or fill out contact forms. Others get drafted into the process by taking a standardized test, such as the PSAT or PLAN. In either case, once a student is in, watch out for the avalanche of college mail. For a high school student unaccustomed to getting stacks of letters, there can be a feeling of instant popularity. How many students have been contacted by a Stanford or an Oberlin and have concluded, "They must want me!"

College admissions offices can send mixed messages. Up to the judgement day of the decision letter, we seem to smile at each and every applicant. Then we turn on the frown and cease all contact with most of our applicants (perhaps even 90 percent of them), sending a brief and vague rejection letter that conveys a message between the lines: you were not quite good enough for us. Certainly no college comes right out and says that. Most speak euphemistically, referencing the curmudgeonly "admission committee," citing the vast number of applications received for the "limited number of spaces" available. Every admissions dean has sent such letters. Many of us even received them when we applied to colleges.

Recipients of rejection letters, no matter how unrealistic their prospects may have seemed to objective observers, are often stunned. Just ask anyone who has been a high school guidance counselor during the month of April. I have been there. As a counselor, I felt the pain. As an admission dean, I have caused the pain. Along the way I have often thought that if colleges communicated to prospective students and parents more like a neighbor chatting across the back fence, rather than like a politician spinning to advantage, we might be seen as more trustworthy.

I suspect that prospective students and their parents wonder sometimes whether admission deans are educators or sales managers. We can seem like masters of the bait and switch. While engaged in recruiting mode, colleges and universities send letters and email containing near promises of admission. The biggest tease letters go out in "the search," to PSAT, PLAN, or ACT takers with high scores and high grades. Prospective students and their parents probably do not realize that many colleges, Reed among them, sometimes contract out the writing of the search letter to direct mail firms skilled at crafting catchy phrases.

When his daughter was receiving search mailings, *Washington Post* reporter Jay Matthews observed that students may feel "courted then dumped" by colleges that pursue applicants initially, then turn them down later. Matthews' article referenced a sentence from my own search letter for Reed College: "Listen: college admission people all over the country, including me, have decided that you are the kind of smart student they want." Matthews also cited an Ivy League University that sends a window decal for prospective applicants to "display proudly." An odd practice, considering that the University in question denies 90 percent of its applicants. Should that University's rejection letters include a utensil for decal removal from the family car's back window?

Matthews asked if I would ever revise a letter or brochure if applicants and their parents found it misleading. In fact, the Reed letter he quoted was one I inherited and authorized, with minor revisions, during my second week on the job. Reading Matthews' article, I became concerned about the implied message in my letter. So I revised the letter to read, "colleges and universities—Reed included—are already vying for your attention, proclaiming their offerings." The new sentence, I hope, is less of a tease.

Colleges are places of learning, where students and faculty commune with ideas. But colleges, like all non-profit organizations, face bottom-line pressures. Prospective students and their parents need to understand that all admissions communications, from web sites to view books, reflect institutional self-interest. Colleges and universities want to provide stimulating and vibrant educational environments, so they seek to attract bright, motivated, talented students who, collectively, bring diverse backgrounds and interests. Because we believe that high-quality students seek high-quality institutions, we promote our best features.

Perhaps the most controversial and high-profile aspect of institutional self- interest concerns the students we admit. Who gets admitted and why? The simple answer to that question is the applicants we want the most. But colleges and universities seem to say, or imply, that only "the best" or "the most qualified" get chosen. Does every (or any) college simply admit the most qualified applicants? Who defines most qualified? During my stints as an administrator at Bennington, Vassar, Duke, Boston College, Oberlin, and Reed, I have seen, in nearly every case, a version of admission by category, with the categories determined by institutional needs and priorities.

Most applicants compete not with the whole applicant pool but within specific categories, where the applicant-to-available-space ratio may be more, or less, favorable than in the pool at large. Categories can exist for athletics, ethnic diversity, international citizenship, institutional legacy and loyalty, musical and artistic needs, component schools or special academic programs, and in some cases, even gender. Students in the selected categories, which vary from institution to institution, have a "hook" because they help meet institutional needs. Books such as Elizabeth Duffy and Idana Goldberg's *Crafting a Class*, former Stanford admission dean Jean Fetter's *Questions and Admissions*, and former Santa Cruz, Vassar, and Bowdoin dean Richard Moll's *Playing the Private College Admissions Game* peer into the hidden reality of category admission.

If we want to provide useful back-fence counsel to prospective students, we must be frank about category admissions. The public is shrewd enough to extrapolate from books like Jacques Steinberg's *The Gatekeepers* the reality that most applicants are "hookless" and thus in fierce competition for a limited number of spaces, once the institutional priorities are filled. Our candid explanations of the reality of selective admission can help prospective students understand that behind every rejection letter, whether stated or not, is the undeniable fact that the candidates selected best matched the institution's needs. Admissions decisions are not random or arbitrary, but neither are they infallible or exact science. Sometimes we grossly underestimate the talent we see before us; I think of the student I wait-listed at Oberlin who went to Reed and earned a 3.6 GPA and a student I counseled who, after being spurned by Stanford, went to Washington University and became a Rhodes Scholar.

At the risk of redundancy, I need to say again that there are no random or arbitrary decisions in selective college admissions. Every decision is discussed, sometimes again, and again, and again. Still, annually I encounter at least a dozen students who tell me some version of the following scenario: "I am going to apply to the University of Ultra-Selectivity and Prestige, even though I know I have no chance to get admitted. I know it sounds crazy, but maybe when the committee gets to my application, the dean will be asleep, or they will flip a coin, or they will stamp my file accept instead of wait list or reject." Sorry to break your illusions, prospective students, but just as there is no Santa Claus or Easter Bunny, there is no random quirk of fate that will overrule the reality of transcripts, test scores, essays, recommendations, and institutional priorities.

Do all colleges and universities practice category admissions vigorously? No. Most colleges and universities are not ultra-selective. Many quality colleges admit students up to the first day of classes. Even when practiced, the category admissions approach has different impacts from institution to institution. Major state universities, for example, reserve slots for recruited athletes but in aggregate those slots are a small percentage of the incoming class. Assaults on affirmative action have all but closed an explicit ethnic diversity category for state colleges. A few small colleges lack varsity teams and face no pressure to favor alumni children. Small colleges rarely admit students to individual departments or schools. Yet there is no avoiding the daunting fact that the most selective colleges and universities pose an admissions challenge—where applicants outnumber available spaces by multiples of ten or even twenty to one, category admissions cuts an unforgiving swath.

What does all this mean for confused prospective students who simply want to get a good education? It means you need to keep your options open, because there is no way to guarantee that you have what your first, second, or third choice college wants. That is not as bad as it may sound, because if all you want is a good education (and you want that more than you want a brand-name degree), you can get a good education just about anywhere. It also means rejection is less about you and more about the college or university doing the rejecting.

Remember that well-used breakup line, "it's not you, it's me"? This time, it's true.

The Rank Lyrics of the Sirens' Song

Sean Callaway
Director of College Placement and Internships, Pace University
Center for Urban Education

"The purpose of education is lost to prestige in ranking recruitment wars."

It's called college admissions—a billion dollar industry. Society expects untried and insecure adolescents to be responsible for $150,000 purchasing decisions while under the duress of the sugar plum visions from sophisticated marketing campaigns selling prestige, fun, and livelihoods. Parents are convinced that the sticker from Prestigious College glued to the rear windshield of their family car is the Good Housekeeping Seal of Approval. Teachers, counselors, and peers exclaim, "It's a great school."

Newspapers reported Senator Bill Bradley's SAT verbal score to be less than 500. Were he five-foot seven inches, would he have become a Princeton Rhodes Scholar? Once, I asked my teenage son why one student from his high school had been admitted to an Ivy League school while another, who had much better credentials, was rejected. He told me that even though the first boy hadn't taken his studies quite so seriously, he did play great third base, and the school had just graduated its third baseman.

My son's insight wasn't his alone. It was common among his peers who were in the throes of applying to college under fierce social pressure. These kids were convinced a game was being played and that they knew only some of the rules. Hidden agendas determined their admission into the few schools that supposedly would guarantee them successful lives.

Properly understood, admissions is rational—that is, institutions attempt to act with rational self-interest though not necessarily in the best interest of adolescents. The driving force that has turned admission into a feeding frenzy is the miracle of scarcity, an artificially induced scarcity driven by sophisticated marketing in times of increasingly difficult economic conditions for post-secondary education. It isn't fair, but it is real.

There is no objective basis for admission to American colleges and universities. While there is data available about each candidate that informs admissions decisions, these decisions are made within institutional guidelines about how the student body should be crafted. Therefore, preferential admission is basic to college admission, and preferential admission has five essential characteristics.

First, every educational corporation has a business focus that informs admissions decisions. Educational corporations cannot educate if they cease to exist. Classes are crafted around institutional needs to stay in business and stay competitive in institutional peer and public perception, especially in light of the looming health-care-like financial crisis and consolidation facing American higher education.

Second, admission isn't personal. It's about enrolling classes, not individuals. Well-rounded classes are being seated, not necessarily well- rounded students or bright students. And lacking an objective basis for admission, the overall profile (known as the profile of yield) of every class is an outcome of institutional policies. Institutional policy frames and weights how applicants are perceived.

Third, the segmentation of the admissions pool reflects institutional goals for the profile of yield. While not quotas or separate admissions pools, segments are institutional targets for the profile of yield. Segmentation means that academic comparisons are very important, but they come into play first within the segment of the applicant pool in which the applicant is perceived to be, and then in relation to the overall strength of the admissions pool in light of the relative importance of the segments to the institution. This can be seen clearly in different rates of admissions for different segments based on institutional needs (for example, athletic, legacy, minority, geographic). And within segments, often times, academics are not primary. For instance, should an institution take an All-American high school basketball player with lower SAT verbal scores or a player who is isn't as good but has a much higher SAT verbal score? Segmentation can occur in a variety of ways, but generally, in every situation where there are fewer spots in a class than applicants, segmentation occurs.

Fourth, supply and demand of applicant characteristics determine institutional selectivity, and these are linked to the segmentation of admission pools determined by institutional policy. Applicant characteristics include family assets and income, athleticism, race and ethnicity, geography, gender, alumni and social connections. Grades and SAT scores are very important, especially in conjunction with denial rates and yield rates which all impact internal measures of success, rankings, bond ratings, and interest rates.

Fifth, admissions is based on the basement threshold. Every institution has a bottom threshold below which an applicant will not be admitted unless overwhelming pressure is brought to bear (such as a seven figure donation). The class is admitted from students who exceed the threshold. Reality is that if one's credentials are above the basement threshold, then one is just as admissible as anyone else. A class is not built top down from requirements hung from skyhooks. It is always built bottom up, which is how, in this real world of economic and social gravity, everything is built. For a variety of reasons, however, institutions pretend, in public, that classes are hung from "merit" skyhooks rather than built bottom up. We have no standard national high school leaving exam, and if we did, it would reflect the historic condition of rich and poor school districts. And, while the SAT is bogus as a "merit" measuring stick because it only partially correlates to success in freshman year, it can be useful as part of the application package because GPA, in this era of high school grade inflation and bizarre class ranking, is also suspect.

Historically, post-secondary institutions have been vague about how admission really works because, from an institutional perspective, admission is concerned not with "merit," but with peer institution and public perception of academic selectivity, and with the profile of yield. The more selective the perception, the more selective is the reality—with eventual ramifications in Wall Street bond ratings, interest rates, the ability to compete for star professors, and a favored place at the federal trough. Admission is key to winning in the institutional wars.

The economic dynamics that drive institutional competitiveness are not going to go away because we wish it so. Economics are not going to permit the overthrow of enrollment management. Clearly there is a legitimate and necessary ranking system for colleges and universities—Moody's Bond Ratings. And that ranking system does pay attention to the number of applications, denial rates, and yield rates as part of its analysis. Lie to Moody's and you will pay.

What should be happening for the high school student? It is a time of growing self-awareness, a time of empowerment to put education into an adult perspective leading to the end of childhood, leading to separation from parents and individuation. Insofar as adolescent self-esteem is manipulated and destabilized in the admission process, and parental common sense is undermined, post-secondary institutions bear a considerable moral responsibility. The illusion of scarcity and the pressure of prestige can be mitigated. While the competition among institutions will not go away, we can dispense with some of the trappings that harm the development of adolescents for whom admission is always about access. While the public is not really interested in education as much as it is in professions, networking, and jobs, it should be in everyone's interest that learning once again is stressed as a significant reason to attend college.

It is of paramount importance that high school students don't feel excruciating pressure to go to certain schools or else their lives will be over. Upward mobility doesn't depend on admission to a handful of schools. In trying to market themselves as selectively as possible, in cooperating with ranking systems, post-secondary institutions ensure students will be driven into emotional frenzy, and this not by accident.

Students from more affluent background seem to have some understanding about how early decision, denial rates, yield rates, SAT averages, segmentation, and interest-based admissions impact their chances. They may feel admission to the fabled fifty or the favored one hundred is the only thing preventing socio-economic and social disaster. These students often are desperate to be among the angels sitting on the head of a pin.

As a generality, middle income students and students from competitive public high schools also seem to have some understanding of how admission works. But added to the stress of getting in, for them, is also the stress of paying for it. Far too many of these students appear to be extremely upset: academically driven for the sake of sufficient aid dollars that only a proportionate few may get.

Students from lower socio-economic strata have the glass ceilings of rank and prestige pressing their self-esteem into the ground. Frequently, they feel like losers before they have even begun. There is a crushing weight of low expectation laid upon them.

One bright spot in the admissions game is that minority students are learning how it is played. It can be quite liberating for them. Currently, minority students (though not necessarily Asian students, who often are "over represented") are at a premium in crafting classes. One of the consequences of the segmentation of the admissions pool is that the admission of minority students has had relatively little impact on the overall rates of admission of European-American students, because these groups are in different segments and often are not directly competing.

But minority admission has had a significant impact on the matriculation of poor European-American students. Money is tight and it is a definite factor in admission and yield—even with legacies. Only so much money is available for the poor, and minorities are over represented in poverty. This, of course, has resulted in pitting the poor against the poor. Our inability to expand equal opportunity has been hidden behind the smokescreen of litigating affirmative action.

The business imperatives, the focus on classes rather than students, the segmentation of the admissions pool, varied applicant characteristics, and the basement threshold will continue no matter how we calm the admission waters. Educational corporations need a variety of incomes and aptitudes, not just intellects, to stay in business. Rankings assuage faculty egos, inflate alumni chests, reassure trustees, and smooth the path of the development specialists. But when post-secondary educational corporations, building on parental, high school, and peer pressure, knowingly induce fear and emotional stress to create a sellers' market and drive the supply of applicant characteristics, *it's immoral*. While it may make good business sense to use every tool of predictive modeling, one-to-one marketing, and sophisticated emotional market manipulation to land the yield, from the point of view of fostering the growth of adolescents in cognitive and affective maturity, it's cannibalism. Fundamentally meaningless ranking systems tied to early decision, denial rates, yield rates, SAT averages, and interest based admissions *are immoral*.

The purpose of education is lost to prestige in ranking recruitment wars. Education becomes a thing to be measured and weighed. Admission is the message we send to teenagers, and they come to understand that their life is a market place and college is just one more product. Their lives are things to be bartered and spent. Students are taught that education is not the primary interest of colleges and universities. The message is that the purpose of human life is utilitarian rather than liberal. While perhaps only about one hundred institutions in this country profit from this game, all the other post-secondary institutions have to commit to it in order to keep up with the big guys and to stay in business. But there is no such thing as being a little bit pregnant.

Abandoning rankings is not going to end public perception or marketing, but it will quiet things down. Adolescents and their parents need more space for reflection. There will be opportunity for institutions other than the favored few to be seen as great life opportunities, rather than as failed back-windshield stickers. And it will end some of the pressure associated with early decision, with demonstrations of interest—other than the application itself—as a condition of acceptance. It will mitigate parental, peer, and high school tunnel vision about "right" schools. These are good reasons to end the rankings race. But more than anything, colleges and universities will exercise the moral leadership that is obligatory to their identity when they stress by example that being educated is more important than having a degree, that action is not more primary than being.

And the lesson can be taught. But, while many of our educational leaders deplore the admission and ranking frenzy, their institutions profit from it. There are far too many presidents saying they wish something could be done about the situation, but nothing happens other than talk. Lip service is paid to the goals of non-commercialized admissions and educational choices. It was reported that when Frank Sinatra was making one of his many farewell tours, Luciano Pavarotti visited him in his dressing room at Carnegie Hall. Sinatra, who always worked on his lyrics, told Pavarotti that he was having trouble ending his musical phrases and getting on with it. He asked Pavarotti for advice. Pavarotti replied, "Just shut your mouth."

And do!

If the schools of the Ivy League, the Claremont Colleges, the New England Small College Athletic Conference, and the University Athletic Association—which combined represent fewer than thirty-five colleges and universities—were to agree that they would no longer cooperate with organizations such as *U.S. News & World Report*, and that they would try not to generate admissions feeding frenzy, the ranking system would be partially discredited in the public eye. The public relations momentum generated by promoting education rather than commercialization would be great. It would not end commercial systems of ranking. These grow like weeds from the human desire for pride of place to hide deficiencies in self-esteem or to secure material advantage. But the momentum would force the post-secondary world to give some important moral example about priorities. It would give voice to the primacy of being and to the primacy of the transmission of life at the very moment when the sirens sing to our children.

Editor's Stories II

"When rankings become important for self-measurement, management of an institution's image becomes driven mainly by external factors."
Steven Koblik, former president of Reed College

During the 2002 - 2003 school year, a record number of colleges employed outside marketing firms to help enhance their institutional images. Knowing that many of the highly paid marketing consultants had gotten their starts as educators, I wondered if the call of education might still resonate in their professional lives—at least enough to let me ask a few questions. I discussed this idea with a few of my admission dean colleagues, and sure enough, I was referred to a VP of one of the largest enrollment management firms in the country. My phone call provoked a predictable immediate response from the executive, followed by a very intriguing willingness to reveal.

"Why are you talking to us?" began his response. "We are the enemy."

"Well," I replied, "I want to believe that we are all educators at heart."

"It's too bad that is not the case," said the executive. "There are more freshmen than ever before, more dropouts than ever before, and more consultants than ever before. We are selling things which can't be justified educationally."

Without further prompting, this veteran executive and embattled former educator began to divulge instances of educational transgressions with an apparent sense of confessional relief. There were the stories of colleges advertising majors for which faculty were suspiciously scarce—in one case, a major was promised by a department consisting of only a half-time professor. Many customized and expensive college brochures inaccurately portrayed colleges with less than authentic pictures, lists of campus activities, and descriptions of courses. At some colleges, courses described in the catalogues had not been taught for a number of years. Statistics about schools, such as graduation rates, job placement, average standardized test scores, the number of applications received, and retention rates—all numbers which could be fudged—were. Many newly manufactured college images, ones ostensibly more attractive to a wider range of students, were developed using these kinds of strategic tactics. The stories continued as the executive began warming to the purpose of this investigation. Then suddenly, as if shifting into self-censor mode, he ended. "It seems that the new field of marketing education has yet to have its ethical boundaries defined," lamented the vice president as he hung up. In that moment, I remembered the ordeal of one of my most ethically driven friends under the pressures of competing values imposed by enrollment management strategies.

John, an admission dean at a liberal arts college, struggled while working with his college's president, an ambitious, shining example of the new breed of the college CEO. These presidents are relative short-timers, averaging five to seven years at the helm. They aggressively seek to improve the reputation of their colleges by appealing to the rankings; they promote an image of the college as they envision it, not one of the college as it is; they allocate resources, employ market strategists, and try to diffuse campus tension in their focused zeal to gain status for their college.

Amid rising faculty suspicion of this unprecedented presidential prerogative, John struggled to serve his president's ambitious agenda. During the next few years, the coordinated management of admission and financial aid activities would be used to achieve the expressed presidential vision of increasing the college's reputation. This required using scholarships to attract those students whose SAT scores and GPA's could be attractively reported to the ranksters, and demanded a major shift in the college's financial aid program—from one that had been entirely need-based and intended to increase educational opportunities for students to one that increasingly relied on scholarships to attract student stars. Initially subsidized by a $400,000 grant to the institution procured by his predecessor, "the new president got sufficiently addicted to the practice," according to John, that soon millions of dollars were redirected from need-based awards to the scholarship program. And, eventually, a new strategy called "leveraging" was instituted—a practice of strategically discounting the price of college for students who can pay their own way to help subsidize the expanded scholarship fund.

While John never believed the rankings had much value, he was committed to his college and he wanted to support his president. Perhaps there was a more direct and less educationally disruptive way to improve his college's rank, John thought. Using his research skills, his personal contacts, and diplomacy, he arranged to meet with an editor and reporter from *U.S.News & World Report* and his president. The goal was to demonstrate that the magazine's rankings disproportionately favored east coast and midwest colleges in their "Top Forty" list; that this did not serve the circulation interests of the magazine; and that his west coast college certainly deserved to be included in this ranking. Although John had been struggling in his relationship with the president, this particular venture appealed to this executive officer of education. The following fall, his college appeared for the first time in a *U.S.News & World Report's* list of top colleges. The president was quite pleased with John—even though the category had now grown to include fifty colleges.

John was able to endure another year of his president's meddling as CEO in admission. Eventually though, all remnants of the student-focused, admission counseling model that John had worked for ten years to build were gone, replaced by what was becoming a "standard industry management strategy model" for improving reputation. And it gave John little comfort when a highly regarded academic statistician commented to him, "This is the story of thousands of colleges; it is why the educational disparity between income levels has grown so drastically among college-age students." This fact was confirmed by a summer 2002 *New York Times* article describing how financial aid resources have been radically shifted from lower income students in order to attract higher paying, higher achieving students: "The whole issue of access for low income students has gotten lost in a race for prestige."

From another college comes a similar story of president as entrepreneur. Soon after arriving on campus, this president created a new executive position, Director of Planning, and hired a person with an exclusive marketing background. This was accomplished quickly, and without the typical university committee involvement. The new Director of Planning immediately convened a committee on image and marketing and recommended that the president send out an RFP (request for proposal) to the top five college consulting firms. The RFP was drafted and signed by the president; it described his interest in wanting to "increase the college's image and ranking most expeditiously." Again, with uncharacteristic lack of regard for campus input, the president selected a firm whose proposal's price tag exceeded $800,000. Without any guarantee of return on investment, the firm proposed work and costs in the following areas: Market Research—$150,000; New Publications Series—$350,000; Web Redesign—$125,000; New Capital Campaign Development--$150,000; Public Relations Outreach and Media Management—$100,000. While these numbers may seem astounding, the proliferation of college marketing and branding agencies has increased threefold during the past four years.

Practical Perspectives: On Choosing the Right College

Richard H. Hersh
Former President, Trinity College

"Far too many incoming students choose their colleges for all the wrong reasons.... It doesn't have to be that way. You do not have to play their game. It is your education...."

Far too many incoming college students choose their schools for all the wrong reasons:

It's where their parents went, or where their parents wish they went. It's close to home.

It's far away. It's prestigious and expensive. It's good enough and it's cheap. It has a great football team.

The fact is, like most big decisions in your life, you don't get to know you made the right choice when you set out to college that first day. That will be determined by what you do when you get there.

As a result, you, and what you bring to your undergraduate years, are the most important variables to consider when you choose a college or university. It may be a cliché but there is still no better advice to give to a student than "be true to yourself." The school you choose is only part of the equation. You are the other part.

Because choosing a school involves entering into a personal relationship, you cannot pick the right college or university off the shelf. An education is a process, not a commodity. Unfortunately, the admissions process in America today has become so commercialized and competitive that it makes "shopping" for the right school seem like a high pressure game show in which one "lucky" person wins big prizes and everyone else loses. It's such a compelling metaphor that many parents, and students, even many schools, are sucked into it.

It doesn't have to be that way. You don't have to play their game. It is your education, after all. I would go so far as to say don't go to college right out of high school, if you are doing it primarily because of your parents or because all your friends are going. Far too many students spend the first two years of college with very little personal understanding of why they are there, and are too easily distracted by the sometimes dangerous diversions that will be available to you on campus. If you don't want to go to college right after high school, take a year off, work, travel, volunteer, breathe a little. College should be something you do with a purpose, not a shrug.

Claiming your right to make your own decisions about your education, of course, means that you won't get to blame anyone else for making poor choices on your behalf. Once you opt out of the marketplace mentality that surrounds college admissions, then you have to accept that when it comes to your education, you are not the "customer" and you are not "always right." Now you are responsible for your own choices and what you make of them.

And, the fact is, the choices you will have to make are not clearly defined. Such basic information as what is the fundamental purpose and value of a college education has been so distorted by the hype surrounding college admissions as to be unintelligible, if not unrecognizable.

What drives the conversation about quality too often are ratings like those found in *U.S. News & World Report,* which, over time, have come to be sanctified as if they actually stood for anything. In fact, the rankings in *U.S. News* are highly predicted by one statistic: endowment per student. If you know a school's endowment per student ratio, you have a pretty good sense of where a school will rank. Endowment per student ratios, however, do not tell us what, if anything, is actually being learned in those schools. The rankings are based entirely on input variables, not learning outcomes. Take away the packaging and it is obvious that the whole ranking system is just a way of selling magazines and playing to the mass-market, "learning mall" mentality. Don't rely on a magazine to choose a college.

A "practical" education

There is a popular sense today that there needs to be a practical or utilitarian purpose for education. Following that logic, most people see higher education as little more than providing a passport to the workplace. A graduating student is thought of as a finished product: ready to work. That's actually a fairly naive notion in this day and age when you can expect to go through many changes—each requiring different skill sets—during the course of your career.

If we broaden the definition of education to providing us the opportunity to continue to grow, value quality, and discover a passion for learning—all the things that a liberal arts education does—then a liberal arts education can be seen as "practical" in a much deeper and wider sense than the way most people use that word to describe education today.

Ironically, the people who understand this attribute of liberal arts are neither students nor educators. A national survey I commissioned a few years ago, completed by social observer Daniel Yankelovich, polled five different categories of stakeholders in liberal arts: the parents of incoming college students, incoming students, current students, graduates of liberal arts colleges, and the CEOs of businesses that hire college graduates.

In general, the parents of incoming students thought the highest purpose of higher education was having their son or daughter land a good job. Incoming students tended to agree with their parents. Current students and recent graduates showed a slightly greater appreciation of the value of their liberal arts education.

The surprise in the survey came from CEOs, who very clearly identified the knowledge and skills associated with a liberal arts education as the most practical preparation for a long, varied, and successful career. They look for graduates with a liberal arts background, they said, because they know they will be able to grow and change as the demands on them change. They know they will be able to think independently and yet work well in teams. They can be focused, but they can also see outside their specialty. The CEOs we surveyed say they want to hire people like that.

Greater Expectations

You have a huge array of schools to pick from today; besides the Ivy leagues and the big name research universities, there are literally thousands of institutions to choose from that each offer different educational environments. The abundance of opportunity is daunting by itself, but it is better than the popular misconception that there is only one school out there that is right for you.

Higher education in America is going through some major changes and understanding them can help you see your choices in a broad context. One of the best ways to get that perspective is by checking out a major analysis of higher education in America that was released last fall by the American Association of Colleges & Universities (AAC&U). A national panel of educators, of which I was a member, worked for two years on a comprehensive report called "Greater Expectations: A new vision for learning as a nation goes to college." (The study is readily available online at www.greaterexpectations.org.)

The gist of the report is that although the network of colleges and universities in America have been able to dramatically increase access to higher education, the quality of the education that is available today is not as high as it should be. The report takes its name from the observation that schools should expect more from their students than they have in recent years. For this essay, I would note that the converse is also true: Students should expect more—insist on more—from their schools.

The attributes of an excellent education are well known. Whatever your chosen course of study, when you are selecting a school, look for one that demonstrates these values:

High expectations and high standards. Many studies have confirmed that expecting more from students contributes directly to higher levels of learning.

Emphasis on high academic engaged time. There is no substitute for time spent learning a task (at the appropriate level of difficulty).

Frequent assessment and prompt feedback. Assessment can take many forms, from short quizzes to long papers. It can be written or oral and doesn't always have to involve a grade. Without it, students have no measure of their own progress.

Active student engagement. Learning occurs best when students move out of a purely receptive learning mode (e.g. a lecture hall) and into one in which they actively operate in and on their environment. Discussion, individual or group projects, laboratory work, tutoring others: all require active learning.

Frequent contact with faculty. Interacting with faculty in and out of class increases the probability of student risk-taking, useful feedback, greater clarity of learning objectives, and a greater sense of student connection to the school.

Individualized learning. Students enter college from different backgrounds, and with different interests and competencies. Learning is enhanced when institutions and faculty respond to the individualized needs of each student.

Collaborative learning. Working in student teams, peer tutoring, and student study groups outside class enhance problem solving and communication skills, provide immediate assessment feedback, and promote respect for different points of view. Collaborative learning at school is a lot like lab work for future employment.

You may have to dig through the admissions brochures and review books to find these attributes, but your search will be well worth the effort. If you don't find these values in those materials, ask about them in your admissions interview. And, if you still don't find them, don't go to that school.

Because you want to be

Here's the bottom line. Find the very best, the most demanding schools you can get into, and then go to the one you fall in love with. No matter which school you select, there will come a moment fairly early on when you're convinced you made a mistake for any number of reasons. At that moment, it is important to be able to say, "I made the decision, not my parents or anyone else. I chose this place because I wanted a place that would be demanding, I had faith in, and would challenge me. I'm here because I want to be."

You can make a mistake; that's not the issue. Becoming liberally educated, in fact, could be seen as figuring out how to turn your mistakes into learning experiences. It is that skill, more than any other, that will set you free.

Admission Selection: Discerning Intrinsic Talents in a Confounding Era

Karl M. Furstenberg
Dean of Admissions and Financial Aid, Dartmouth College

"...college admissions has become the setting in which our society is working out the tension...between the deeply held American values of merit and fairness."

College admissions selection has become a highly complex, controversial, and political subject, particularly regarding the most competitive colleges. Underlying this development is a growing tension between the deeply held American values of merit and fairness. Definitions of merit and fairness vary depending upon one's place in society and particular stake in the admissions process. Many populations not traditionally included in American higher education want greater access, while, at the same time, groups that have benefited from relatively easy access want to preserve that advantageous position. To a significant degree, college admissions has become the setting in which our society is working out the tension between these values. Nowhere is this more evident than in the debate about affirmative action and the resulting University of Michigan case in the Supreme Court. Public discussions and concerns about legacy and athletic admissions, as well as the controversy over early admissions plans, all demonstrate the keen interest in the means and manner by which students are admitted to college and university.

Gaining admission to college has clearly become a more competitive, confusing, and anxious process for today's high school students. Intense marketing by colleges and universities, aided by direct mail and the Internet, has surely contributed to a significant surge in interest in selective colleges. More fundamentally, though, this phenomenon seems driven by our society's insatiable appetite for quality and status, leading many students to focus on the schools deemed to be the most selective and prestigious. Nowhere is this more evident than in the focus on annual rankings published by *U.S.News & World Report* and other magazines and guidebooks. In our increasingly competitive and fast paced environment, there is a very clear public perception that attendance at an "elite" college gives an individual an edge in the economic, social, and cultural mainstream.

The growth in the size of applicant pools has been accompanied by a surge in commercial organizations that offer services to assist students, families, and secondary school personnel with both the admissions and financial aid transition from secondary to post secondary education. Many students and families now view such services as necessary to success in gaining admission to a "top college." Some might argue that the explosion in applicant pools is at least partly due to the prevalence of such services that heighten the general visibility of the admissions process. One ought to at least ponder this relationship with some skepticism, because the organizations offering these services have a vested interest in generating more activity around the admissions process, which creates more demand for their services. Even if a correlation cannot be made between the availability of these services and the growth in applicant pools, it seems clear that this has definitely contributed to the "mania" in certain communities. Too often, these services focus on ways that students and their families can "beat the system," as opposed to encouraging students to engage in a thoughtful reflection on their strengths, talents, goals, and aspirations.

Also raising the visibility of the admissions process are the various media outlets, which seem to be constantly producing stories that either focus on the difficulty in gaining admission to college or purport to reveal some "secret" about the inner workings of admissions. The distinction between the media and college preparation services has become blurred because several of the major providers of such services are now owned by major news media organizations which are, in turn, part of larger business organizations: hardly a formula for objective news reporting free from conflicts of interest. All this taken together has the unfortunate effect of focusing too much attention on the admissions process, making students and families unnecessarily anxious. Many secondary school personnel lament the degree to which all this college angst is undermining true learning during the high school years.

This era of applicant pool growth and the resultant competition for admission has been accompanied by an astounding increase in applicant diversity. Students from the widest possible range of intellectual interests, leadership in extracurricular and community involvements, socio-economic circumstances, nationalities, racial-ethnic identities, geographic origins, type and quality of secondary schools attended, and parental educational background are seeking admission to America's finest colleges. As such, selective colleges are no longer the exclusive province of our society's wealthiest and most privileged citizens. In a very real sense, selective admissions has become a more pluralistic and inclusive process.

The dramatic shift in the size and composition of applicant pools, facilitated by expanding financial aid resources, has necessitated a multi-dimensional approach to admission candidate evaluation. Dealing with such diverse applicant pools defies the use of formulas, fixed criteria, specific weighting of various factors, or segmenting the applicant pool into groups of "similar" candidates. Given that most students who now find their way into selective college applicant pools are well prepared to experience academic success at our colleges, admissions officers cannot rely upon simple formulas of class rank and/or grade point averages and standardized admission tests to make decisions that are informed, equitable, and appropriate. Truly, there are no longer any absolutes in selecting students. Instead, the complex and highly competitive nature of our applicant pools requires an in-depth review of each applicant because each student represents a unique mix of life experiences, values, ambitions, and abilities. For some colleges, including Dartmouth, this involves a process known as holistic evaluation and individual consideration.

Holistic evaluation entails consideration of all aspects of a student's background and accomplishments, utilizing many different sources of information. These sources typically include biographical information, student essays, a transcript of academic work, standardized test scores, recommendations from teachers and counselors, and, in many cases, personal interviews. Each of these "reference points" provides added depth for our understanding of candidates and helps admission committees discern the true meaning of a student's credentials. In the end, holistic evaluation attempts to understand the authenticity of talent, accomplishment, and potential in the context of background and opportunity, or lack thereof. Individualized consideration refers to the fact that individual applicants are considered one by one on their own merits and judged against the overall criteria for selection, never as members of a subgroup or category within the larger applicant pool.

The consideration of student background factors is an underlying tenet of holistic evaluation and individualized consideration. Background factors provide the context in which to evaluate student achievement and potential. A highly selective admission process is all about context, since context is the only way to equitably, thoughtfully, and accurately evaluate candidates. To evaluate credentials without context is to judge them in a vacuum, devoid of meaning and substance. Holistic evaluation seeks to understand the available resources and opportunities that shape each applicant's experiences and development.

The consideration of background factors has become increasingly important precisely because of the way in which commercial college planning services have entered in as a confounding factor. The prevalence of coaching and other services that prepare students for the admissions process are a reality which cannot be ignored by admissions committees. Stories of $100 per hour counselors "sculpting" kids' resumes abound. And access to these services is not equitably distributed across the applicant pool. A significant correlation between SAT prep services and socio-economic background exists. Admissions committees, therefore, cannot ignore or overlook this fact and be fair to applicants, let alone be successful in admitting the students with the greatest intrinsic accomplishments, talents, and potential.

A fundamental dilemma that faces any selective admissions process is whether or not it can ever completely "level the playing field." It is ironic that some who complain the most about the use of context in making admissions decisions are very often themselves subscribers to commercial services which tend to inflate the assessment components used in the more formulaic admission selection process. Many of these applicants feel entitled to admission by reason of their numerical credentials and having compiled the "right" resume sure to impress the most jaded admissions officer, never stopping to think what circumstances and advantages might have given rise to those credentials in the first place. Increased competition among students leads them and their families to seek an edge and advantage. Those with resources and interest will always have an edge, or figure out a way to gain one, no matter how the system is structured. Nonetheless, colleges and universities should do all they can to structure selection processes in a manner that maximizes the possibility of recognizing the intrinsic talents, accomplishments, and potential of applicants, regardless of background factors that might disproportionately advantage or disadvantage certain students.

The pursuit of holistic evaluation is the means by which admissions committees can introduce equity into the difficult choices that must be made, equalizing to some degree the disparities of opportunity that exist across an applicant pool of tens of thousands of competitive students. It is only through this time-consuming and painstaking process that we can work toward the ideal of admitting the most talented and deserving students with the greatest potential to benefit from our educational programs and serve our society in leadership roles.

Higher Education: The Status Game

William Adams
President, Colby College

"College and university leaders must do all they can to resist the status game. We must resist the temptation to make important decisions to improve our ratings and rankings."

By April, most high school seniors across the country have received their admission decisions from the colleges and universities of their choice. Some celebrate. Others feel a deep and personal sense of rejection, which is troubling.

The higher education choices offered in America are unrivaled in the world. There are nearly 4,000 community colleges, four-year colleges and universities, enrolling almost 15 million students. Over the last two decades, however, we have become less eager to celebrate this abundance of choice. Prestige has become the coin of the realm in college selection and marketing, and both prospective students and institutions are competing more and more aggressively for a greater share of that most rare and alluring of all commodities in higher education—reputation.

Part of the reason for this shift can be found on campuses like that of Colby College, where, in subtle and overt ways, prestige has become integral to our identity. Our students and their parents want to hear—and are told—that they are several cuts above the pack. Our college magazine features stories that foster pride of affiliation among alumni. Our handsome admissions publications imply, in statistics and in prose, that only top students need apply.

Part of the reason can be found in the ever-increasing horde of college rankings and guidebooks. The best known of these is the annual *U.S.News & World Report* guide to "America's Best Colleges," but there are many others. Some, like *U.S.News*, rely on statistical analysis to reach their conclusions, though the value of this methodology is hotly debated among educators. Others, like the Princeton Review's "The Best 345 Colleges" guide, combine statistics with commentary that is, at best, unrepresentative of students and, at worst, mind-bogglingly superficial. (The University of Vermont is No. 1 on the "Birkenstock-Wearing, Tree-Hugging, Clove-Smoking Vegetarians" list; Reed College tops the "Students Ignore God on a Regular Basis" list.)

But at least the Princeton Review does a few hours' research on campus, gathering anecdotes from students. By contrast, Kaplan's "The Unofficial, Unbiased Insider's Guide to the 320 Most Interesting Colleges" is apparently written without benefit of a campus visit. Careful readers of the breezy report on Colby in these pages will discover, tucked away in the margin, the advice that, "If you love the great outdoors but don't want to become an alcoholic," you should attend another school. It's glib. It's entertaining. But does it serve any purpose beyond making money for its authors and publisher?

The best of the college guides can be valuable tools for helping students and their parents navigate the sea of choices. For instance, if a student knows that she wants to study at a small college in California and is leaning toward a career in oceanography, a guidebook will assist her in narrowing her choices. But no rating or ranking can tell her whether a college will suit her individual needs. Only careful research can do that.

Even though we know that rankings have only the slimmest relationship to what we actually do, college and university administrators have become deeply complicit in the ratings game. Schools that make SATs optional to boost the mean score of the class they admit surrender to the rankers. So do those that put a ceiling on numbers in seminars to affect average class sizes as counted by *U.S.News*. Complicity is a disservice to our students and prospective students, and it helps distort various public policy issues affecting higher education.

Some things can be quantified, and certain quantities matter. Money, for example. Prospective students and their parents can reasonably compare the wealth of one institution to the next and the effect of that wealth. Other quantitative measures—student/faculty ratio, number of classes run by teaching assistants, or average class size—can be helpful in forming general assessments of institutions.

But the "unmeasurables" matter far more: How extensive and deep are the programs of particular interest? What is the campus climate and culture? How committed is the faculty to teaching?

Answers to these questions do not lend themselves easily to simple scales or hierarchies. Like marriage, choosing a college is as much about complex questions of chemistry and fit as it is about abstract attributes that can be measured and summed up to produce a quantitatively satisfying outcome.

Can we regain a healthier perspective on the college admission process and improve the decision-making of prospective students, parents, and institutions?

I think we can. But we need to be prepared to abandon the notion that the qualities of a particular institution can be summed up and translated into a prestige rating. As nice as it might seem to stressed-out students and their parents to simplify college selection to some cookbook recipe or statistical formula, we need to return the focus to where it belongs—on the individual needs and characteristics of the student, and on how those attributes align themselves with the complex attributes and opportunities that different institutions present.

For our part, college and university leaders must do more to resist the status game. We should speak out, clearly and often, about the traps of rankings and rating schemes, and we should insist that the helpful and necessary work of college guides and our own marketing efforts be focused on descriptions of what we actually do, not how we rate. We must resist the temptation to make important institutional decisions to improve our ratings and rankings. The good of our students and our institutions, current and future, must be the goal of our decision-making.

You Must Re-member This

Ted O'Neill
Dean of Admission, University of Chicago

"What happens when we reach a point when a membership organization is no longer operating in its members' best interests, but in its own interests?"

I have been asked to write about The College Board in the larger context of my own outspokenness about the increasing commercialization of the college admissions profession and process. The College Board is not the sole culprit in the changes that carry us, and our children, away to a place not many of us would knowingly choose to be. No one really wants ideas and decisions and young lives to be for sale, but much in the modern world (one would once have said, not so long ago, in the modern American world) has conspired to make the mercantile model *the* model of our time and the foreseeable future.

What has brought us to this point? Paradoxically, we may have been enslaved by freedom and free markets, by the manipulation of our wants in the market place, and by the market place's reliance upon currency and standard of measurement. The Enlightenment—the movement which freed us from superstition and kings, and in the process assigned everything a name, a weight, a number, a price, in order that our reasoning could make plain sense to any other rational being—has prevailed. Along with this enlightenment has come democracy, and the rationale for the claim that all people are created equal, and the associated claim that our lives, liberty and the property—goods and ideas and talents that define our lives—are our own and inviolable. Naturally, we would not have things any other way.

The College Board, and the Educational Testing Service, are the most important institutions in the modern American effort to measure the mind and its products. The SATs have become the instruments we most frequently rely upon for the measurement of something variously described—aptitude, developed ability—not always the same *thing*, but at least a thing consistently measured. In our age of enlightenment no one wanted to rely on the old methods for determining worth: being the son or daughter of the right parents, being rich, being righteous. So, The College Board was invented by us, and we set about believing in it and its tests. Then, somewhere along the way, the Board and ETS, or we as members, decided that an education in this country would be more accessible and negotiable if a college education could be defined, analyzed, and sold as AP courses. Why romanticize college education? Romance is, after all, antique and relates to mere human story-telling. Write a test, teach in order that the test can be passed, and the test score would measure the worth of the experience, which can be equated to tuition money saved. AP tests and scores can be counted and rewarded, and then college faculties could take the AP scores and total up how much of their work had already been done, how much higher education had happened.

Feelings about the Board have roots in politics, which is only to say that feelings about the Board can be complicated. We want to belong to an entity which has the power to ensure that we live in an orderly society; we willingly give over some freedom to an organization which maintains order, issues coin of the realm which has legitimacy and uniform worth, and tells bad people — racists, fat cats, nepotists, elitists—that they can no longer have their own way. However, we do not like big organizations telling us what to do, or assigning value to things we care about deeply. Insofar as the Board loses its claim to be a membership organization, a claim it states with such numbing frequency, insofar as their coinage (SAT scores, AP courses, grades for good writing) is debased, or called into serious question, and insofar as its rhetoric (its heart, to harken back to that unenlightened organ) is betrayed by its actions, then the Board stops being the body to which we truly belong.

When did the shift occur that began to move some of us away from our sense of true membership in the Board? There was never a time when everyone was entirely happy with the Board, and I remember even at the first National Forum I attended in 1981, observing a rebellious fire on the floor, especially at the College Scholarship Service meeting (in the days before the assembly meetings were show pieces, and when people really were given a chance to talk.) I was introduced to the Board by my friend and mentor Dan Hall, who in the days of my first Forum, was on the CSS council. A populist himself, a Lutheran minister's son from Nebraska, Dan truly believed in what we used to call the "level playing field"; that is, he did not think the playing field was level, but could imagine that it could be leveled with the proper instruments. Financial aid was his instrument, and the Board was his ally. As a first time attendee at National Forum (the Forum! ... the assembly of the people!) I was not too dazzled to be amused at the splendor of the meeting place, the Waldorf Astoria Hotel. We came in from around the country and were treated to the Waldorf! I remember the opulence of the suites occupied by Board officers, and the relative grandeur of Dan's room, his by virtue of his position in CSS. A lot of men in suits seemed to occupy the back wall of every meeting—not the sport jacket informality of NACAC. One felt vaguely impressed, vaguely under the scrutiny of those suits.

The Board, and ETS, have been criticized for extravagance, but the bread and circuses of the Waldorf years seemed a reasonable enough reward for the faithful. And the Board and ETS themselves deserve their nice quarters, and good art on the walls, and high salaries—they are truly important people attempting important work. Much has been made by some of the high living of those in charge of our membership organization, but there is also some comfort in the fact that our people live like the real bosses. However, the event that stands out as different, as too much, as a turning point, was the moment when the Board made a tactical error, at the meeting those of us present will never forget, when Gaston Caperton announced that we had amassed a surplus of $100 million and then led us off to the top of the World Trade Center to have a party.

It was a great party. Champagne and open bars and dancing until late at night at the top of the world, the top of American and world commerce, just like the fat cats The College Board was established to supplant.

Perhaps it was just too much, or perhaps it was just that the new leadership was no longer embodied in Don Stewart, a true educator, a genial man, a guy from my own neighborhood, and in the people I had come to know and like. A new team had come on, and their style was different. College Board might have always been more Cambridge, New York, Washington, D.C. than it was Holdridge, Nebraska, or the South Side of Chicago, but educators, wherever they are from, do share some things in common. The bottom line is different, and has to do with learning, not profit and not power. I think at that point I began to feel like someone along for the ride, not a member, not one of the people in the forum.

A side note about being along for the ride. First, I was someone who liked testing because I did it well, so testing helped me and I was grateful. I believed that the tests were designed to give everyone an equal chance, and were a measure of an individual's brainpower. CSS made sense to me, and still does. I loved the chance to get together at the Forum with admissions colleagues, better yet with those old friends plus financial aid people and academicians and high school teachers and counselors. As a college teacher, I never quite bought the whole AP venture, though I realized then and now that the AP has helped many schools and teachers and enriched many students. Somewhere along the line I was asked, and was pleased to join the Board's Membership Committee, and then the Bok-Garner commission to examine and recommend changes to the SAT. That was when I first supported, and then heard the objections to, the inclusion of writing in the SAT. So, though I once indelicately made reference to the fact that so many of us have found ourselves "sucking at the Board's sugar titty," I meant it in part as a confession. I accepted the Board's largesse, and having accepted the stature afforded by these positions of honor and the rewards, feel a bit like a heel for being critical now. Of course, it is a membership organization, and members should get out from behind the plough every once in a while and go to the capital to take a turn being a general or legislator. But if we are not speaking about an actual membership organization…

After checking out the views from the Windows on the World, word came down that The College Board, the membership organization, would simultaneously be a for-profit company, collegeboard.com. What did that mean? Who proposed this astounding hybrid? Who would the investors be, and what, in addition to profits, would the investors expect? How would the investors, and the search for profits, determine Board policy? We were told that plenty of investors were out there willing to buy in. Why? What did the Board and ETS possess that would so interest investors? Well, thanks to the members and their SAT I, SAT II, and AP policies, most students and virtually all colleges and high schools, members or not, must use College Board/ETS services. What is the cost to students and families? The cost of the exams can be staggeringly high for many families (with the promise of great savings resultant from shortened college careers, though those savings rarely seem to be realized). A more substantial cost may be extracted silently, by way of "voluntary" offerings of personal information and the right to privacy. Our membership organization, for awhile non-profit membership/for-profit dot.com, now asks all students registering for the SAT, for example, to become members too. As members, they get to register for exams the other members, the colleges, insist they take. As the new "member" fills out the membership application, some required information is collected, and then the member rolls into the spaces for voluntary information. Do they realize how valuable that information is to a commercial operation, either officially for- profit or not-for-profit? Does this sound like a monopoly, propped up by the admissions policy of member institutions?

In short, the Board seemed more and more to be about marketing and revenue generating, for a time boldly as a dot.com, but still unrelentingly as a not-for-profit. We had to go dot.com to generate enough funds to compete with Princeton Review and

Petersons, etc., but what then differentiates our for-profit from theirs? Presumably, the difference is that our operation is run by educators, theirs by businessmen. Is anyone comfortable with that explanation? Was anyone comfortable with the thought that a monopoly established through the collusion of the colleges and high schools would now own information about millions and millions of students, consumers, and would sell them advice about the tests the Board commissions and controls, and counsel them about getting into member institutions, and so forth?

There no longer is a dot.com. Does that mean that marketing efforts have subsided? Every time there is a new Board forum, National or Regional (and now, with the overwhelming Board presence—short-lived, one hopes—selling goods through NACAC "panels"), new schemes emerge for the selling of more things. A plan to offer lists of students who should be taking APs but who are not, with more rebates built in for schools with more test takers; an "AP diploma" that would pretend to rival a rigorous and coherent curriculum like the IB (more tests sold); and who knows what next? Just today, an announcement arrived, ill-worded and ill-conceived, that The College Board is "rolling out a new brand and is branding—is branding—is branding." Is this education? Is this English?

What happens when we reach a point at which a membership organization is no longer operating in its members' best interests but rather in its own interests? At the very least, one pulls back in some dismay at the promise that has been betrayed. Or, as many of us observe in our own offices and schools, we resentfully rely, because we have no alternative, upon what once was our own but is no longer. If the social contract is abrogated, and our relationship to our organization becomes one of a consumer relating to a producer, then one understands why what once may have been a forum now becomes a stockholder's meeting...or sales meeting.

The next metaphor, that of the "coin of the realm," would have test scores, SAT I and II and AP, seen as our medium of exchange. College Board/ETS goes to painstaking, exacting care to be as sure as possible that scores consistently mean the same thing across time. What do they mean? Anyone in the public would imagine that we could tell them exactly what scores mean to *us*, even if we could not articulate what they mean in some greater vision of the ultimate success or scholarship or happiness of test takers. Most admissions officers base their allegiance to the tests on research the Board/ ETS offers which proves that scores add a bit of power to predict first year grades in college. Do we ultimately care, when we make admissions decisions, about first year GPAs? Would substituting, say, family income or the educational achievements of parents in place of SAT Is or IIs predict first year GPAs as well as SATs do? Would a more thoughtfully designed application predict first year grades, or even more meaningful college success, better than SATs presently do?

We all, students and schools and admissions officers, go to a lot of trouble, even anguish, to attend to these tests and scores. Do we know why? Perhaps the scores are necessary because they provide an objective, external measure of … what? If we cannot supply a good answer to that question, we can at least take comfort in the "objectivity" of the exams, the faith that the scores are the one element in every application which are comparable across applicants, states, and schools. Can we state confidently that scores are comparable across the lines of social class, or, let us say, family income? No, we have known better than that for a long time. At some point, we, and then the Board, had to face the issue of whether coaching could increase test scores. The Board/ETS fought for a long time to prove that coaching did not matter, or not much. I remember talking to Dan Hall at NACAC about what he would say when he confronted Jonathan Katzman of the Princeton Review in a session at NACAC. At that point, Katzman was the devil as far as admissions officers and counselors were concerned. He, in effect, sold knowledge, and did so gleefully, which would lead to higher scores. We were morally outraged, realized with sinking hearts that our argument was based on something like, "But we really *want* these scores to be meaningful, objective, and integral to the test taker, even if we know, in our heart of hearts, that they are not." We were naive, but our practices have not changed as a result of what we have had to accept.

When I was a member of the Bok-Gardner Commission, I was surprised by the allegiance of some very important members to the value of SAT IIs. In the Midwest, where the SAT IIs are seldom required, it seemed ridiculous to expect SAT II scores to attest to anything but the power of the school at which the test taker was educated. But SAT IIs were good predictors of college grades, so many did, and many do, think three or five SAT IIs are appropriate measures of the worthiness of a college applicant. Yes, true, if redundancy is the key to selecting students who are most worthy. Be born to the right parents, live in the right neighborhood, go to the right school, do a good job at your right school, and you have a good chance of succeeding (getting A's) in college. How much does the Board/ETS profit from the sale of SAT IIs now that they, in addition to SAT Is, are seen by many to be necessary to our work in counseling and admitting students? Why not just skip the tests and assume that families who can afford to live in a good school district can afford coaching and testing and re-testing, are likely to have children who will do well in college? In lieu of the tests, the Board should simply become a bank, into which families deposit money to establish their child's worth. We shall have a membership commercial bank.com.

AP scores have been sold as equivalent to passing grades in college courses, as free passes worth so-called "sophomore standing" (for having tested out of the first-year experience?), as a way to save thousands of dollars in tuition. How many families save thousands of tuition dollars thanks to APs? Next to none, in my 23 years at one particular, and particular kind of, college. How much do people pay for the privilege of taking the exams? I remember writing the checks for my son and daughter, and the amounts were not trivial in my family—how much does it hurt most families in America to come up with those fees? The push for more and more APs is relentless. In the end, do APs help the educational effort? They may, and perhaps the reason the scores represent both money and a tangible, measurable advantage in the admissions process is to goad students into more rigorous course selection. But if the score of four or five is supposed to mean that a student had had the experience of sitting in a college classroom with college students and a professor and learning within a college environment, then someone is being sold a bill of goods. The fact that amongst those someones are admissions officers and college faculties, who cannot resist the temptation to trade their academic autonomy for more applications and higher yield, does not entirely excuse the salesmen of the tests.

The very thought that test results should determine a child's future is a particularly un-American notion. However, politicians who, in the name of freedom, refuse to extend health benefits to the entire population, or to raise the tax burden on the wealthiest members of the society, and conspire to reduce Pell grants, seem perfectly willing to have government impose exams to determine who deserves one of the most valuable goods in our society. Imposing exams means imposing a curriculum. American higher education is as good as it is because colleges have developed according to the dictates of their own goals and principles, and have escaped the dictation imposed by a national curriculum or canon. Academic freedom, in combination with America's enormous wealth, has made American higher education the envy of the world. Even at the primary and secondary levels, local people have insisted upon the right to make decisions about how their children should be educated. If each school district were equally well funded, perhaps primary and secondary education would also be the best in the world, given the power and promise of local interests and local ideas. Now, for many good reasons, but also because those with the most power have children who are most likely to do well on their exams, we watch as tests establish curricula and pedagogy. The more we institutionalize exam results as the measure of the intelligence, diligence, the worth of a child (and the value of teachers and schools and communities), the more we invite the creation of a hierarchy in America, a country thus far free of institutionalized inequities, with the glaring and terrible exception of the experience of African-Americans, the more we violate our abhorrence of imposed, official distinctions amongst our people.

Who came first, those who insist on testing or the test-makers and test-salesmen? Let us just say that the truly difficult and fine work The College Board/ ETS has done in assembling testing instruments, in combination with their lobbying and marketing efforts, have convinced educators and other interested parties that the tests meaningfully evaluate students, schools, and districts. And, the test makers and sellers are not shy when promoting the argument that if you test for it, whatever the "it" is, it should and will be awarded value. Should we, as citizen educators, accede to the equation of knowledge and learning to measured results? Most of us say no, and yet still require the tests. Can we, for now, delay the loss of local freedom to a corporate power, e.g., Federal government, state government, The College Board? Probably. But we cannot ignore two things: one, the likely outcome this kind of incessant testing, sorting, and labeling will have in a society not equally in possession of opportunities and wealth; two, the way the enshrinement of testing changes the nature of the educating moment.

Back to my own eye-opening, and entirely pleasant, experience on Bok-Gardner. Many of us around the rather large table believed that learning how to write was one of the absolutely crucial goals to be achieved in a successful education. The then SATs, now SAT Is, required no writing, which seemed odd if the tests actually tested developed aptitude, not simply aptitude. Therefore, we asked if writing could be adequately graded in a consistent way, and we were assured that at some cost it could be, and we seriously entertained adding a writing sample to the SATs. However, a California contingent argued forcefully against the writing sample, and threatened to pull California out of SAT testing entirely if writing were to be included in the exam. The grounds of their argument rested upon the assumption that, as important as writing is, a writing exam would surely discriminate against ESL students and, indeed, against any students whose language background was likely to be less embedded in standard American English. They were, of course, right. The writing exam would reify the already dismaying discriminatory effects of the testing already in place. Their arguments were good, and they were the California market—they won.

Apparently, as the story goes, California has won again. Now California insists upon the writing exam, and we will get it. Has anyone successfully refuted the argument that the writing sample will put ESL, first-generation English speakers, some African-Americans, most poor kids, at yet a further disadvantage? California is a bellwether and is also rich and powerful. We have frequently looked to California for guidance in ways to educate a large, diverse public. Now it appears that it ignores its own reasonable assessment of the writing sample and we, of necessity, must go along. Who can forget the president of The College Board, at the National Forum, telling us that he could hardly care that little Mt. Holyoke had stopped requiring SAT Is, given the fact that the Board had just sold the entire California system on the idea of requiring SAT IIs from all students applying to a California public university—*all* students? Can you imagine the value of that single sale? How many families pay how much money so that how many kids can spend how many hours proving the fact that if you go to a good school you are more likely to get higher scores? Who would care about Mt. Holyoke, a tiny college for women, in the face of that commercial bonanza? So, despite the unfairness inherent in the writing sample, we are in effect told that as good admissions officers we have to make silent adjustments, see through the unfairness, act affirmatively. And we certainly will, as we always have when regarding SAT Is, IIs, and AP scores—as long as the courts and the public and our faculties and boards agree to let us do so.

The writing sample, because it must serve a very wide audience in conditions not conducive to the production of good writing, will surely be an instrument without any real discriminatory power in selective admissions. The essays' prompts are sure to be insipid lest too many test-takers be confused or put- off. The grading will of necessity be formulaic, which means the teaching of writing will become formulaic. We will enter the era of the SAT essay as the standard for adequate American writing, and then goodness help us. The teaching of truly good writing will be squeezed out of the school day by the teaching of writing-for-tests. The writing sample is to be a sample of first draft writing, not writing by which any writer would willingly be judged. The advantages to well-schooled children will be immense, and even those not well-schooled, but affluent, will surely be able to buy coaching for this most easily coached of all test segments (the most difficult segment to coach, analogies, will be dropped). For the suspicions amongst admissions officers, the writing sample will offer a chance to compare the writing we receive in the application to an unrevised, hurried, cautious sample, though even the most paranoid will have to have too much time on their hands if they feel they can add this extra step to application reading. Despite these obvious and unanswered criticisms, we are urged to support the new exam if we truly really care about writing in America. This moral suasion, offered by some of my most respected colleagues, loses some of its appeal when accompanied by the Board's insistence that we insist that ACT takers be required to include a writing sample lest the Board lose business. After all, the Board is us, and our tests are better and deserve *our* support.

Nonetheless, even the writing sample is earnestly supported by educators as well as the test salesman, and will be composed as competently as such an instrument of limited promise can be composed. The Board's/ETS's exams are good, well-calibrated, and constructed with care and with a sharp eye to eliminate questions that obviously favor one racial group over another, one gender over another. I had a brief stint as a test item writer-in-training back in the early 80's, and the people involved in test design and constitution are obviously well trained, smart and dedicated. Much, if not all, of any criticism leveled thus far against the tests is really based upon a challenge to the salable pretense that the inequalities and unfairness of American society (the most equal and fair of all modern societies) do not matter when it comes to testing. The main force of any criticism of the Board may well be fueled primarily by our impatience with the zealous marketing of tests and all the attendant services that are now sold so eagerly. The marketing is annoying and unseemly and alienating, but that is all just business, if not just education. However, we must consider now the permanent damage that might result from ETS's triumphs in test design, and the Board's power to market exams as real measures of real human worth.

The Board is actually at its best when promoting awareness of racial discrimination and its effects over time. Once you get past the annoying sloganeering that infects Boardtalk—"equity and access, excellence and equality"—you can see that the organization is interested in promoting opportunities for underrepresented minorities. After having attended the national and regional forums this year, I am almost convinced that Brown v. Board of Education was a College Board production. Some of our profession's most earnest defenders of affirmative action are in the employ of The College Board. I do not think the Board's commitment to racial equality can be questioned. However, the marketing of Board products, including the tests, undermines the very "equity and access" the Board promotes (and does nothing at all for excellence).

Given the tremendous campaign to convince us all that SATs, SAT IIs, APs, and writing samples are absolutely crucial when judging young people as college candidates; given the collusion of the test marketers and the politicians who cry out for "standards"; given the insistence that the tests are, if no longer coach-proof, "objective" in some important way; given these givens, can we blame a public for thinking that we are admitting the wrong kids if we ignore the evidence of test scores? The Board absolutely needs affirmative action (as does the nation, for real and good reasons) because without a legal justification for *ignoring* the results of tests, someone might believe we should actually take them seriously all the time. The tests must simultaneously be understood as absolutely essential *and* as inconsequential. How long will the state legislatures and courts buy that? The more precision attributed to the tests, the more ammunition critics of affirmative action will possess for their fight for "fairness" and "objective standards." In order to adhere to the evidence the tests provide, we tacitly agree to punish poor kids—notably, but not only, white kids from bad schools who test poorly and who are not in the spotlight of affirmative action—and then agree selectively to ignore test scores for the sake of affirmative action. But every time we admit someone with low scores we are forced to think we are making an exception or granting a favor. This suggests to me that a reasonable, thoughtful evaluation of applicants which emphasizes the essential and de-emphasizes the most obviously socially constructed aspects of the applicant is in danger. The danger comes from the test marketers, co-opted through a desire for profits, unwittingly in the service of politicians who most need the myth of genetic, or racial, or class superiority.

As for the educating moment and that is which is essential: at the last National Forum, The College Board, bless them, introduced me to Anna Deavere Smith. In her dramatic depictions of Studs Terkel and James Baldwin and Margaret Mead and Cornell West and the rodeo rider from Idaho, she did more to help her audience understand people and their intrinsic worth than would hearing the words "equity and access" repeated two million times. She actually gently chided the Board for its tests and the advantages they convey to the already advantaged, but it was in her call for a slow consideration of people rather than a measurement of people that she really, subversively, moved her audience. That lesson, of course, was for us in the admissions and guidance world, but one can imagine that it also was directed to her host, The College Board, most especially. Is it time to say that some of my most respected friends work for or have worked for The College Board? That in many ways we could not get along without it? That CSS is a vital and necessary arm of our effort to educate students without obvious regard to their ability to pay? That, without question, many students, teachers, and schools have benefited from the AP programs which have, in some places, set goals that have pushed education along to new levels of excellence? That, despite the fact that I feel I must wear a suit rather than a sport jacket to the various forums, I learn from the people and programs? That I, too, have enjoyed my stays in the Empire Hotel and nice meals at The College Board's expense? The College Board *is* us, though I think lately we have let ourselves be herded in directions we would not, as responsible educators and citizens, wish to be driven. Once again a healthy and concerned opposition seems to be forming, which might make this membership organization a membership organization once again.

Editor's Stories III

"This is total craziness...The kind of unscrupulous behavior which has characterized some admission offices has now moved to the level of college president."
Dean of an Ivy League college

"We spend about $3,500 to attract and enroll each student—and that is on the low side compared to many of our competitors."
Dean of a liberal arts college

The 1980's has been described by one marketing expert as the "decade of the child consumer." During that period, Madison Avenue began to scrutinize and pursue children with intense and focused efforts. Major ad agencies established children's divisions; new firms emerged to focus solely on kids; and new industry publications were established to cover the latest ad campaigns and market research. The logical culmination of these well-orchestrated efforts to increase both current and future consumption can be seen in the mass "customerization" of prospective college students. Last year more than three hundred registered college marketing and branding agencies enriched themselves to the tune of more than $1 billion by reducing students to customers as they sold marketing services to colleges. Here the most "sold-to" generation in history has been primed to view college as the ultimate purchase, and to respond with predictably characteristic consumer behavior.

Before leaving my counseling job in February, 2004, I probably could have filled my office five feet deep with the direct mail advertisements our 250 seniors received from colleges. Imagine 500 cubic feet of highly produced brochures and personalized letters—all strategically packaged to invite consumer response. Considering that the cost to produce and mail these materials exceeded $100,000, and that The College Board charged the colleges approximately $25,000 for the names and addresses of these students (after being paid by the high school to collect the names and biographical information as part of the PSAT), there is a lot of money being spent to attract students at my school. Considering that there are approximately 2.5 million high school seniors nationwide attending some 20,000 schools, the marketing of colleges has become very costly.

Last year more than 100 college recruiters visited my school during a two-and -a-half month period. The costs associated with this activity probably exceeded $20,000. Then there were college fairs, alumni interviews, evening presentations at local hotels, well-orchestrated telephone and email correspondence. Thanks to the information collected by The College Board when students register for the PSAT and SAT, colleges know more than ever about high school students, and they do all they can to respond with personalized marketing tactics. The bottom line at my school, roughly calculated, was that each of our students was probably chased by colleges at the cost of $5,000 per student. Very few students reported to me that they were positively impacted by any of the colleges' sophisticated marketing efforts. In fact, most of the stories I heard were to the contrary. And yet admission/marketing budgets at many colleges have nearly tripled during the past ten years, supporting increasingly questionable recruitment strategies. The experience of one particular student being "hustled" by a college bears recounting.

Since her sophomore year, colleges had their sophisticated marketing eyes trained on Erin Hill. PSAT scores and grades, all reported via registration for the PSAT, helped The College Board sell Erin's biographical information to more than 1,000 colleges. At 25 cents per name per college, this is big business. As a result, Erin, along with most of our students, had been receiving daily mailings and emailings from colleges, scholarship search services, financial planners, and credit card purveyors. Her name had gotten out there, with mesmerizing results. Like thousands of other students in the commercially transformed college admissions process, Erin had been treated as a targeted consumer for a long time. This treatment puzzled her parents, who had intentionally chosen a rural life to escape some of commercialism's influences. Their encounters with the "customerization" of their daughter as a prospective student led to many discussions with me about maintaining educational focus. But even my special relationship with her parents and my own experience with marketing education had not quite prepared me for the most recent episode in the Hills' saga.

"Last night the president of 'X' college called," said Erin's mother, Mary, as she uncharacteristically closed my office door and sat down. I moved around from behind my desk and leaned forward, anticipating something meaningful. She continued. "Now please do not repeat this, but the president asked Erin what colleges she was considering. After she told him her choices and reasons for the choices, the president said that although he did not like to do this, he was going to grade the colleges she was considering. Accordingly, one of her colleges he would give a grade of 'B,' another he would give a 'C,' and the other, well, he said he could not even give a grade to that one. Of course, his college got an 'A.'"

Silence. The look on Mary's face, a face I had seen express so many emotions during Erin Hill's four-year educational experience here, was a combination of defeat and sadness. I was stunned. Recoiling, I instinctively searched for counselor tricks. Was there a way to put this into context, to glean knowledge from everything we had learned over the past four years of discussions about college admissions?

Without a word, we shook our heads; we nodded our heads; she left.

College Admission: As If Learning Mattered

Michael Beseda
Vice Provost for Enrollment, Saint Mary's College of California

"Learning, especially liberal learning, has little to do with rankings of colleges and the bumper-sticker mentality of so much of college admissions."

The best college application essay I ever read was also the shortest. Twenty-three years and many thousands of applications ago, I stumbled upon a gem. In the days before personal computers or even word processors, Saint Mary's College of California, like many other schools, included a blank sheet of paper in the application for prospective students to either type or write their essay by hand. The brief instructions at the top of the page asked applicants to explain why they wanted to attend college in general and our institution in particular. In the middle of this sheet the applicant, an average student from a large public high school in the Midwest, neatly printed the following: "I want to learn."

One four-word sentence and nothing more—that was the entire essay. Even as a rookie admissions officer, the audacity of this offering stopped me dead in my tracks. It forced me to think. What could this mean? Was she making fun of the application process? Protesting having to write an essay? Was she taunting us? Or had she really identified something fundamental about the collegiate experience? Was this a moment of clarity, an epiphany about the real and ultimate purpose of the college? My more experienced colleagues in the admissions office shared my bemused reaction. With our dean, we agreed she was worth a risk, if for no other reason than to find out what was behind that koan-like essay.

Long before she graduated at the top of her class, received the College's highest academic awards and starred in several college dramatic productions, this student understood in a direct and powerful way what college could and should be all about—learning. And most importantly, she acted on that understanding.

In the commercialized world of college admissions where attending the "right" college seems increasingly about prestige, rankings, athletic programs, campus amenities, or making the social grade, I am dismayed by the lack of emphasis on learning. Ask yourself the following questions: Do colleges primarily market themselves based on the kind of learning community they provide? Are admissions decisions made on the basis of fit between an applicant's desired learning environment and the institution? Are colleges ranked based on their students' learning?

I have a genuine bias; college is primarily for learning, and not just any kind of learning. It is liberal-arts education, or liberal learning, that can distinguish the collegiate experience and make it uniquely valuable. Other kinds of learning—discipline-focused, technical, or career-oriented—have specialized schools or institutions in which they are nurtured and flourish. A high school classroom, trade school shop, or graduate seminar may elicit occasional moments of liberal learning; nonetheless, the educational focus, setting, and level of learning at the collegiate level provide liberal-arts education with a home. Most importantly: If it doesn't happen in college it isn't likely to happen elsewhere.

Many prospective and current college students (not to mention many institutions of higher education) confuse liberal-arts education with "general education." Nothing is further from the truth. Genuine liberal-arts education isn't general; it is quite specific. Liberal-arts education focuses on root intellectual skills and the fundamental questions and ideas that shape human life. Born out of what St. John's College tutor Eva Brann has termed "radical inquiry," it focuses on "the simple but deep beginnings of things." Liberal learning enables us to analyze an argument, think critically, understand quantitative arguments and reasoning, speak persuasively, and write effectively. These are the skills that help us function effectively in our professions and, more importantly, think through the moral and ethical issues of our lives. They are the tools that guide us in discerning the arguments of a political spinmeister or marketing guru to reveal their fundamental principles and assumptions. They give us the ability to get up in front of a community meeting and argue effectively for or against a community development project. They provide the avenues to engage in dialogue about the value and perils of new technologies. And they are the skills that allow us to think through issues of war and peace.

Where does learning, and in particular liberal learning, fit into the commercialized college admission process of today? Surveys show that most students think of college primarily as a means toward a job, a profession, and an economically prosperous life. College marketing efforts and the related ranking systems contribute to this way of thinking by providing students and families with the impression that matriculation at a highly ranked institution guarantees future success. So, if college is a commercial transaction preparing for a lucrative future, of course rankings are important. And indeed it is true that a college degree is an important avenue to professional success. The prospective student is sent to college to prepare to become a teacher, a politician, a businessperson, or a doctor.

But liberal learning reveals a larger horizon for human life. The goal for our sons and daughters is to become not "just" teachers but educators, not politicians but statesmen, not businesspeople but community leaders, not reporters but journalists, and not physicians but healers. It is liberal-arts education, through its disciplined consideration of ideas of justice, good, virtue, etc., that provides the tools and insights that allow humans to achieve these greater goals. And most importantly, we should send our children to college with the expectation that their education will help them to be better citizens and family members.

Some think of a college admission office as the institution's sales force. While those of us in the field like to think of ourselves as educators and typically take exception to such a characterization of our role, it is really no wonder that we are identified in this way by those in and outside of academe. Don't we put significant

131

resources into market research, send out thousands of brochures to mildly interested young people, and develop tag lines and marketing campaigns, among other activities? I am convinced that our proper task as recruitment staff is to articulate as clearly and concretely as possible the character of our institutions as places for particular kinds of learning.

A few years ago, St. Mary's College seniors reported in the College Senior Survey that they challenged their professors' ideas in class more often than their peers at other institutions. This wasn't surprising, given that the core of our curriculum is a series of Great Books seminars in which faculty members and students are required to pose probing questions to stimulate discussion. Accordingly, instead of using the debased rhetoric that all too often typifies college recruitment presentations (we're in an urban center but our campus feels like the country; we're big enough to be comprehensive yet small enough to be personal; we train you for a successful career and provide you with a broad education; our students have loads of fun but also study very hard, etc…), we simply say to students "If you don't like to ask difficult probing questions of yourself, your professors, and your fellow students, don't come to St. Mary's." Our goal isn't to entice as many potential applicants as possible, but to help prospective students and their families understand the ways in which our school's educational approach is distinctive. Contrary to the simple-minded notion of sales, one of the most valuable things we can do for a prospective student is to describe the distinct nature of the educational experience at our institution so accurately that a student can determine that it does or *does not* fit with their learning goals and objectives.

Learning, especially liberal learning, has little to do with rankings of colleges and the bumper-sticker mentality of so much of college admissions. Colleges have struggled to respond to the public desire for evidence of learning outcomes. Some worthy efforts, such as the National Survey of Student Engagement (NSSE), have begun to look at the behaviors that lead to genuine learning. To get a clearer picture of the kind of learning at a particular campus, NSSE asks students basic questions about, among other items, the number of books they read, papers written, and serious conversations with faculty members and students outside of class.   This kind of information begins to provide colleges and prospective students with tools to have a genuine conversation about learning in the admissions process. At the same time, some may ask if the ultimate benefits of liberal learning can even be measured.

On those occasions when I am talking to groups of students or meeting with a family visiting campus, my comments attempt to hone in on the specific educational character of this institution. Typically, somewhere in the midst of my effort to describe our specific approach to liberal-arts education, a hand goes up with an inquiry. Most often the question is, "What does it take to get in to your school?" It may be that the proper answer to this question should be "a desire to learn."

Thoughts From an Admission Officer Mother

Sid Dalby
Associate Director of Admission, Smith College

"I am saddened by how complicated life is for teenagers today—a vice president at a hot college says that Prozac is the drug of choice on her campus."

A former colleague confided in a conspiratorial tone, "You and I both know that there are only twenty colleges worth sending our children to." While I didn't agree with her, I knew which colleges she meant. This past year, fewer than 20,000 first year students (including internationals) entered them; using her standards, less than 1 percent of college freshmen are attending a *worthy* college. This woman is well educated and well meaning, but in this case, I think she's misinformed; unfortunately, dealing with elitism can be an occupational hazard in higher education.

The truth is that garden variety college applicants often are admitted to many—if not all—of their college choices. *The American Freshman: National Norms for Fall 2003*, conducted by the Higher Research Institute at UCLA, reported that nine out of ten freshmen are attending their first or second choice college. Good—not just great—students are wooed with merit aid and more aggressive, attentive recruitment practices.

I vowed to be rational as I went through the admission process with my own daughter, who began her senior year in high school at the same time an admission guidebook I co-authored was published. Sort of like the cobbler's child with no shoes, my daughter had little interest in any of the tips in the book, even though it was dedicated to her. A procrastinating perfectionist, she waited until the last minute to complete applications (thank God for on-line filing), refused to show up on a standardized test date ("I'm happy with my scores") and when asked if she was anxious about the process responded without guile, "What is there to be nervous about?" Don't get me wrong— she acted out and threw fits about other things (the car, clothes, money, and curfews) and I understand now that those blow-ups were therapeutic for her as she dealt with separation and anxiety issues.

We have a great group of friends that were going through the process with their kids and we swapped war stories regularly. On a dorm tour, one family could barely hear the comments of a tour guide over the sobs of a student on the hall phone telling her parents how much she hated the college. (Their daughter enrolled anyway and is happy as a clam.) After driving hours to visit his parent's dream college, a son refused to get out of the car. One daughter was offered a full merit award at her safety school—her dad promised to buy her a car and send her to Europe if she would enroll. (She wouldn't.)

We weren't particularly neurotic about the process—maybe that's because we're an older bunch with the American Association of Retired People magazine arriving in our mail boxes along with *Seventeen* and *Teen People*. The parents I observed who were most neurotic were the same ones who obsessed endlessly when buying a car or remodeling their kitchens.

The things I learned and believe include:

- Look for the best in every college and you're apt to find it. Each college has unique strong points. Remember what our mothers said: *If you can't say anything nice, don't say anything at all.* I make my daughters crazy when I cheer for both teams at their games—the home team and their opponents. I've always told them that I like to see the sport played well and I applaud good play, regardless of who is playing. I wish more people would root for colleges that do what they do well, rather than being blindly loyal to those with name recognition and a reputation for status.

- Listen to your child. She knows how much competition she can handle at this time and what she really needs to learn. Sometimes less is more. For character and confidence boosting, it's important to determine what place in the pecking order a student needs to be to be firing on all cylinders. For example, a high school lacrosse star could sit on the bench for four years at a Division I school or be a four-year starter at a Division III school. A super strong student might be the teacher's pet in his department at a school ranked competitive but would be one of the medium masses at a highly competitive college. Some students do better with more competition while others wilt. Students can use past experiences to judge what level of competition is best.

- Put a college education in proper perspective. If four years of college are truly the happiest years of life, then for most of us the happiest years will be over by age twenty-two. College is a part of life, not all of life. While choice of major and name recognition may help a student get a first job, qualities including motivation, strong work ethic, communication skills, persistence, ability to deal with ambiguity, emotional intelligence, opportunity, and luck are what move people up the ladder.

- Think long-term, not short. Most of us don't peak at age eighteen, thank goodness. For many people, college is a time to grow up and separate from parents and get ready to live in the *real* world. There's always graduate school for settling down and getting job skills.

- I am saddened by how complicated life is for teenagers today. One of my friends, a vice president at a hot college, says that Prozac is the drug of choice on her campus. Adolescence is a vulnerable time these days and I wish I had a magic wand to wave over teenagers so that they wouldn't be so sad, drink so much, smoke so young, cut themselves, suffer from eating disorders, have panic attacks, become obsessive and unnaturally possessive in relationships, have sex so young, drive so fast, spend so much money, steal from one another, and try to kill themselves. The students applying to college these days have been alive during good and disastrous economic times and have watched acts of terrorism on TV that we, their parents, could never have imagined. There are times when I'm not all that confident about the future. Safety, security, good karma, and faith are better bets than prestige and a diploma from a popular place. On 9/11, people running out of harm's way called their homes and their loved ones; I don't remember any reports of anybody calling a college.

- Don't forget to say thank you. Write to the financial officer and thank her for the generous award. Tell an admission officer how effective the tour guide was. Write to the colleges whose offers you won't accept and thank them graciously. Remember, one person's safety school is another person's first choice.

- As parents, we can talk too much about scholarship applications; we can talk too much about deadlines, campus visits, and prepping for standardized tests, but we can never tell our children "I love you" too often.

Above all, be grateful that our students have so many great choices. Our problems and worries are related to abundance, and that's something to be grateful about, too.

Knowledge for its Own Sake

Colin S. Diver
President, Reed College

"Colleges and Universities are evaluated and ranked, and indeed market themselves, primarily as stepping stones to some extrinsic goal..."

Why get an education? Most people answer that question instrumentally. They view education as a means to an end. The end might be to enter a particular profession, to earn a handsome salary, to accumulate power or influence, or to create things (including ideas) of utility or beauty. According to this instrumental view, education is a process of acquiring the knowledge, skills, credentials, or pedigree deemed as prerequisite for attaining a particular status.

There is another view, a radically different view—one that sees education as an end in itself. According to this view, education is a process of self-fulfillment, self-realization, through the cultivation, cherishing, and love of knowledge. People who take this view rarely ignore instrumental thinking entirely. They, too, care about their careers, their respect or recognition in the community, even their pocketbooks. But those things are, to them, secondary. The assumption is that a life truly worth living is a life of inquiry and discovery—a life of pursuing knowledge for its own sake.

There are many young people who hold this second view of education. They are the high school students who get intrinsic pleasure out of solving the puzzles of geometry or calculus, figuring out how to test a scientific or behavioral hypothesis, relishing the beauty, depth, and ambiguity of a great work of art or literature, digging deep into the historical record to explain an event or social phenomenon. If you have that kind of passion for exploration and understanding, this essay is addressed to you.

In today's competitive, consumerist educational culture, instrumental values predominate. Colleges and universities are evaluated and ranked, and indeed market themselves, primarily as stepping-stones to some extrinsic goal such as career success, wealth, or power. Indeed the emphasis on instrumental values has gone so far as to create the impression that there is no place in higher education for those who care about pursuing knowledge for its own sake.

That would be a false impression. There are colleges that care deeply about fostering the love of knowledge for its own sake. The question is: how can you find such colleges?

First, a word about how NOT to find such colleges. Don't rely on one-size-fits-all rankings. Those rankings are invariably dominated by instrumental values. They are primarily measures of institutional wealth, reputation, influence, and pedigree. They do not attempt, nor claim, to measure the extent to which knowledge is valued and cultivated for its own sake. Likewise, you should be wary of recommendations from counselors, relatives, or friends unless you are sure that those counselors, relatives, or friends share your values. If they view education primarily in an instrumental, bottom-line way, their advice is unlikely to steer you in the right direction.

What should you look for, then? Typically, colleges that celebrate knowledge for its own sake have several distinguishing characteristics that you can look for. No one of these characteristics alone is foolproof, but taken together, they can give a pretty good indication of a college's educational philosophy.

1. A common, unifying academic experience.

In an attempt to remain "relevant" or appeal to divergent student tastes, most colleges and universities have abandoned the required curricula of forty years ago. But a few colleges still require their entering students to take at least one common foundational course, such as Reed's Humanities course and Columbia's Contemporary Civilization course. The contents of such courses vary, but they typically promote the intrinsic view of knowledge in two important ways. First, foundational courses provide a common educational experience that enables students to build intellectual community. Such a community facilitates greater discovery through broader interchange of ideas and insights among students, and even alumni. Second, foundational courses demonstrate the way in which bodies of knowledge, almost like living organisms, build on themselves, stimulating further exploration and discovery. Thus they provide models for the very process of lifelong discovery glorified by the intrinsic model of education.

2. *Distribution requirements.*

One indicator of a college's educational philosophy is its approach to distribution requirements. A purely instrumental approach to knowledge tends to view all academic disciplines as essentially equivalent. In this view, unfettered curricular choice is a default position, if not a positive good. By contrast, a faculty that views education intrinsically is more likely to impose some sort of distribution requirement. The reason is simple: The search for truth often leads down unexpected pathways. One who loves knowledge for its own sake needs to be able to follow those pathways, wherever they lead. This requires at least a passing familiarity with the methods and assumptions of the great divisions of academic knowledge: natural science, mathematics, social science, literature, the arts, humane studies. Distribution requirements help to assure that students will gain that familiarity.

3. *Inquiry-based instruction.*

The lecture is the prototypical method of instruction in the top-down world of instrumental learning. The "conference" (or discussion-centered classroom) is the paradigmatic method of learning in the inside-out world of intrinsic learning. To cultivate a love of knowledge, students should be constantly engaged in exploration and discovery. Students must occupy the center of the educational process and play an important role in shaping, and even leading, the discussion of assigned readings in class. In introductory courses in the natural and social sciences, students should not simply read about research techniques; they should apply those techniques in the laboratory and in the field. In art courses, students should practice the techniques employed by the artists whose works they are studying.

4. Research thesis.

Scholarly research is the paradigm of intellectual inquiry, the pursuit of knowledge for its own sake. Most colleges tout the availability of research opportunities for undergraduates and offer elective honors programs. Schools that are truly serious about research, however, require that all undergraduates engage in a thesis-length research project. Only through such an experience can a student come to appreciate fully the rewards, and challenges, of intellectual discovery. Likewise, by adopting a thesis requirement, a college signals that it has made a commitment to a four-year program of instilling in its undergraduates the skills, aptitudes, and perspectives requisite for engaging in sustained intellectual inquiry.

5. Cognitive evaluation.

A college's grading practices can be a very good indicator of its educational philosophy. Colleges taking a primarily instrumental view of education often emphasize letter or number grades that convey very little substantive information other than how one has performed relative to one's classmates. If education is merely a ladder to success, then all you need to know is what rung you are standing on. Colleges that value knowledge for its own sake, by contrast, emphasize cognitive evaluation. Faculty members provide substantive feedback on class work, detailing strengths and weaknesses, areas needing clarification or improvement, and opportunities for further exploration or development. In such colleges, what counts is how you are developing as a scholar, relative only to your own potential. Each student is his or her own ladder to success.

6. Instruction by full-time scholars.

Colleges can also reveal their educational philosophy by their choice of classroom instructors. Much of the knowledge prized by instrumentalists can be communicated adequately by part-time adjunct faculty or doctoral students. Hence instrumentalist schools often count a large number of such instructors toward their self-reported student-faculty ratios. Schools that value knowledge for its own sake, by contrast, want students to spend their time in the presence of full-time tenure-track faculty, persons who have devoted their lives to the pursuit of knowledge through intellectual exploration, and who can best model that activity for their students.

There are other indicators of the extent to which a particular college is committed to the intrinsic view of education: for example, the percentage of its graduates who go on to get Ph.D.s, the percentage of its students who win highly competitive national fellowships, or the relative lack of emphasis on nonacademic activities such as varsity athletics, fraternities, sororities, and the like. Not surprisingly (given the position I occupy), the characteristics that I have listed describe Reed College very well. Reed is a paradigmatic example of a college committed—and committed solely—to the cultivation of a thirst for knowledge among undergraduates. As such, it illustrates a relatively small, but robust, segment of higher education whose virtues may not always be celebrated by the popular press, but, as this essay demonstrates, can still be found by those who truly seek them.

Status vs. Substance: Is There a Choice?

Robert J. Massa
Vice President for Enrollment, Student Life and College Relations, Dickinson College

"There is absolutely no reason for parents and students to be nervous about the college admission process..."

Setting the stage

I have worked in and around college admission for almost thirty years at some excellent schools: Colgate University and Union College in New York, Johns Hopkins University in Maryland, and for the last five years, as Vice President at Dickinson College in Pennsylvania.

I am also the parent of two teenagers: one who is in her sophomore year in college and another who is a senior in high school and is in the middle of his college search. Neither of my children took SAT prep courses and neither were uptight about the college process. So why have I not pressured my kids (in fact, I "de-pressured" them) to push to the max, to strive for the "top of the top," and to position and market themselves to the so-called "best" colleges? Because I know that of the 2400 four-year colleges and universities in this country, there are at least 50 schools that would be great places for my children—where they can grow and develop; where they can engage; where, with the help of caring faculty, they can find a voice that will serve them well in their future and where they can do so in an environment that encourages risk taking without fear of "blowing it." And these schools do not necessarily coincide with the top 10 as seen by *U.S. News and World Report*. My children and I are more interested in substance than in status.

By the way, my son put me in my place a year ago when I was struggling, with his high school counselor, to find a way to enroll him in honors physics as a junior. While he is not taking SAT prep, and it is not a disaster when he achieves an A- or B+ in a course, I know that colleges look at strength of curriculum as a key component in the admissions process. So the scheduling conflict forced my son to make a choice. The decision was easy after he exclaimed, "Look, Dad. If a college isn't going to admit me because I took honors physics as a senior rather than as a junior, I don't want to go to that college!" Case closed. He was "walking the walk" better than I!

When I speak with high school students, and when I read or see press reports of the angst surrounding the college admission process, I sigh with an "insider's" knowledge of the process at some pretty selective colleges. There is absolutely no reason for parents and students to be nervous about the college admission process unless they decide to apply to a college for the wrong reason—because it is "hard" to gain admission; because it is "prestigious;" because everyone will be impressed. What a terrible way to pursue a higher education, and what a misguided definition of success we have developed as a society. Is it more important to look impressive than to be impressive? Is it more valuable to have a "wow" window sticker than to make the most out of a college experience that actually fits your personality, learning style, and educational objectives?

John Dickinson was the governor of Pennsylvania in the 18th century when the college bearing his name was founded. Coincidentally, his family crest bears a phrase that has always guided me: "To be, rather than to seem." I fear that too many students and their parents are more concerned about seeming than about being. I do not think that they even realize this. But their behavior—stressing admission to the "best" (read name brand) colleges, prepping for the all-important SAT, pushing grades and activities as a means rather than an end, applying undue pressure to win the "prize"—belies the fact.

U.S.News is not the cause of the problem, though their ranking system that has become the "quick fix" of the admission world is partially to blame. Rather, we as parents reinforce the image of success in our children that results in an obsession with name brands from cars to clothes to colleges. How can we halt this?

Know yourself first

An old sketch on *Saturday Night Live* had a TV psychologist respond to clients' differing problems with the same advice over and over again: "Know yourself," she said to her patients, who seemed grateful for this insightful and allusive diagnosis. So obvious yet so often overlooked, this self knowledge is really the first step in the college selection process. While there are several websites that will help with a self-assessment (such as www.keirsey.com and www.act.org/discover), simply asking and answering a few key questions will help get a student started on this essential step.

1. *How do you learn best?*

   Are you an independent learner or do you need direction?

   Example: When your history teacher assigns a paper, do you prefer a general topic that lets you explore and go in any direction you want? OR, do you prefer specific instructions such as "the introduction must be at least a page long in which you state your thesis, followed by three pages of developing your argument, three pages of defending your thesis, and a one page conclusion?"

   Are you inquisitive or accepting?

   Example: If a teacher makes a statement in class, or describes a mathematical formula or proof, do you write it down and move on, or do you prefer to think about it and question the teacher if it doesn't make sense to you?

   Do you prefer to work and learn in teams or by yourself, memorizing notes?

   Example: Do you find that working with a lab partner, where you can learn from each other, is more productive than studying and memorizing lab notes?

Are you an active or passive learner?

Example: Do you learn more by being engaged in the process, where you have to think and are often "put on the spot" by teachers? OR, do you prefer the teacher to simply tell you what you must know to do well on the exam?

Do you prefer a structured or an unstructured learning environment?

Example: Do you need the teacher to tell you exactly what to do and when, in order to pace yourself and learn? OR, do you learn best when the teacher gives you a broad overview of what the class objectives are and leaves it to you to figure out how to get there, asking for direction only when you need to?

2. *How do you interact with others?*

Are you an initiator or a follower?

Example: If you are interested in martial arts, but your school does not have a club, will you start one by getting the support of other students and the school? OR, will you be content to join the wrestling club?

What causes stress in your life and what results in enjoyment and productivity?

Example: Are you fulfilled when there are not enough hours in the day to do everything you want to do, or does that cause you stress?

Do you prefer to interact in organized groups with a purpose, or informal groups to "hang out"?

Example: Would you rather be with a few friends and figure out what to do together, or do you prefer organized activities?

Are you open and tolerant of differences, or do you prefer to be with "people like me"?

Example: If you are a "heavy metal" fan, are you likely to go to an orchestra concert just to experience it?

3. *What are your general educational objectives?*

You don't have to know what you want to major in, or even what you want to do after college. You should, however, know what you enjoy learning about.

Example: Are you more verbal, enjoying more subjective areas such as literature or history, or do you prefer the more quantitative, "concrete" areas of study?

Answers to these three simple questions—how do you learn; how do you interact; what are your general educational objectives—will help you understand yourself, and represent the first step in selecting the right set of colleges.

Get to know a college's "personality"

Colleges have "personalities" like we do. Among the typical characteristics:

Small or large / Public or private

Residential or commuter / rural, suburban or urban

Teaching or research focus

Undergraduate or graduate student focus

Nurturing or competitive environment

Hands on learning, small seminars, and community engagement, or lectures

Diverse or homogeneous population

Big-time athletics or emphasis on the varsity "student-athlete" and intramurals

Large fraternity/sorority presence or predominantly "independent" campus

These are obvious enough, but it is legitimate to ask, particularly with so much being sent to students by colleges, "How do I discover a college's personality?"

1. *Use multiple sources*

   Example: Never rely exclusively on one source, particularly shortcut sources such as rankings, guidebooks, and word of mouth.

2. *Counselors and teachers*

   Example: They can help you develop a list of possible colleges that fit your interests, your style, and your academic profile

3. *Use the Web*

   Example: Among other things, the Web is a marketing tool, so be careful. Glean all the information you can from the main levels of the site, but to really discover a college's personality, drill down to the academic and social department level. See what English faculty are doing in their classes and what students majoring in public policy do as their projects. See how faculty and students do cutting edge research together. Get a sense of how teachers teach and how students learn. And learn about how students run their own organizations by visiting the actual websites of those organizations.

4. *Use email to your advantage*

   Example: After searching the web, email some faculty and students who are doing things that interest you. Also use email to contact your regional (or academic major area) admissions representative and introduce yourself by asking a well researched question.

5. *Once you have done your homework, VISIT*

   Example: After you have a reasonably good picture of how the "personality" and program of a college matches your style and needs, get yourself to campus. Stay overnight, talk with all different kinds of students about their experiences, speak with faculty about their role at the college, and of course speak with your admissions counselor. But if you go to a program put on by the admissions office, take some time to speak with students and faculty who are NOT a part of the program. This will help you determine whether what you are seeing from the program translates to reality on campus.

6. *Be objective in your assessments*

    Example: Don't include or exclude a college from your list because of a good or bad tour guide, because of what your cousin says, or because your friends "never heard of that school." You must take the college as a whole—looking at all of its resources—to see how it meets your objectives.

7. *Choose six to eight "first choices"*

    Example: Joyce Mitchell, college counselor at the Nightingale-Bamford School in New York, tells students that they should not choose a college until the college chooses them. It makes very little sense, therefore, to rank order your applicant group. Instead, select the colleges to which you will apply knowing you would be thrilled to attend any one of them if you are admitted (and if it is affordable). There is plenty of time to "rank order" after admission, but if you select your colleges right, you can't go wrong when the final decision is in your hands.

A final word

Nation-wide, only about half of the students entering a four-year college or university graduate. While the rate is typically much higher than that at highly selective colleges, it nevertheless should tell us that many students select colleges for the wrong reasons. The substance of the experience, and how a particular institution fits student needs, should be of paramount concern. So many students never consider liberal arts colleges, for example, because even the "best" of these smaller institutions are much less visible and well known than their university counterparts. These schools aren't for everyone, to be sure, but they would undoubtedly benefit far more students than ever apply.

We did not discuss "Early Decision" in this essay—that is for another colleague to explore. But suffice it to say that if a student does what I have recommended above, a number one choice could certainly emerge early. If it does, ED may be appropriate—but only if the student has been thorough in his or her work.

The college selection process does not have to be stressful if students and parents focus in on what is really important. In fact, the "top" universities may be the right match, but you are unlikely to know that for sure unless you embark on a fearless path of self-discovery and a probing assessment of institutional characteristics. Once you have done this well, your application set will not only make sense, but you will find that your choices in April are broader and more acceptable than you have ever imagined.

Good luck!

Editor's Stories IV

"The importance of athletics in gaining admission to the Ivy League is so uncanny that we ought to put steroids in baby food."
Mother of a recruited athlete

"Don't you want to capitalize on your investment in sports by using it to get into a really prestigious college?"
Mother (to her daughter)

"Category admission" is the use of institutional preferences when admitting students. As a group, athletes receive more preferential treatment than any other category. I recall, in 1999, being questioned by an admission officer from the group of colleges including Stanford and the Ivy League about my assertion that all recruited athletes to these schools were recruited and admitted under early admission programs. The officer said he was not sure whether competition among college coaches in locking up targeted athletes had gone that far. One week later, the officer called with a polite apology and acknowledgement that all recruited athletes at his college were admitted under early programs.

Recent books, such as *The Game of Life*, have well documented the preferential treatment of athletes in admission, and have questioned this practice on both educational and financial grounds. Yet, college athletics is big business on many campuses—even if not completely successful business. I recall a former dean of admission from Notre Dame saying that every football game generates 1,000 undergraduate admission applications. I also heard similar statements when I worked at the University of Southern California. I remember reading the words of a former president of The University of North Carolina who, when questioned about a deal he had just made with Nike and the growth of athletics in higher education, replied, "It really is all out of proportion to any reason or reality....it's bizarre. But it is part of the American culture, and there is nothing I can do to change that" (*Chronicle of Higher Education,* December 5, 1998).

This "culture" of educational capitulation to commercialized sports is especially harmful when it reaches like a thief into the daily lives and activities of children and families.

"I was forced to play hoops all my life; it was such a selfish thing; I could have been doing so many more meaningful things," confesses a teary-eyed, Ivy League recruit to her counselor, while trying to respond to the early decision pressure from coaches. "I feel like I am having to lie about my interest in playing in order to get into..." In her college recommendation I wrote that she is a stellar athlete and student, but that she should be "recruited" for her character. *Character.* Unfortunately, while colleges continue to extol character building as one of their primary purposes, they are becoming increasingly less willing to demonstrate character amidst rising commercial influences.

And then there is the story of Anton, a nationally ranked rower who claimed to have been admitted under early decision to an Ivy League college with a 3.1 GPA. I first heard this news during a January faculty meeting, along with complaints about Anton's snobbish and inappropriate classroom behavior. Without record of having processed Anton's application, I called the college's admission dean to discuss my concerns. He did some checking and found that Anton had bypassed the college counselor (me) and used his relationship with the high school's academic VP to expedite the processing of his application. The dean was also concerned about this young man's inappropriate behavior and low grades—especially with respect to how this acceptance among so many denials to far more academically qualified students at our school would impact future interest in his college. However, said the dean, reluctantly, "Anton was admitted....There are institutional pressures beyond my control."

Another story about commercialism's "cultural" influence via sports involves a high school coach's involvement in ensuring the NCAA academic eligibility of his star running back. Concerned about this athlete's very low PSAT scores, the coach arranged to proctor an individually administered SAT. A 310 point score increase was achieved! However, College Board policy prohibits coaches from proctoring tests. So the coach asked the high school counselor to sign, indicating that the test was proctored legitimately by the counselor. When the counselor declined, the high school principal got involved and somehow smoothed the waters with The College Board.

Finally, the growth of the club sports and sports agents for children has become a most lucrative commercial response to the perceived importance of athletics in college admission. Many high school athletes have spent tens of thousands of dollars, and sacrificed the benefits of playing several sports, to hone and sell their athletic skills. A mother of a female high school soccer player confided that the costs for her daughter's soccer club activities greatly exceeded the more than $8,000 annual tuition at the private high school. Recently, a sports club director was indicted for sexual misconduct with some of the students. As reported by the press, one of the most troubling aspects of this tragic story was how the promise of advantage in college admission offered by the director obscured parents' ability to recognize his predatory behavior.

What are the chances of a high school athlete becoming a college athlete? A professional athlete? Statistics reported by the National College Athletic Association are as follows:

Among basketball players, 2.6 percent of high school athletes will become college athletes, and 1.9 percent of college athletes will become professional athletes. For football players, the numbers are 6.6 percent and 3.3 percent, respectively. While these percentages suggest seemingly slim advantages for athletes overall, at many of the top-ranked colleges, preference for athletes is significant. It has been reported that more than 20 percent of the students admitted to Ivy League colleges are athletes. In contrast, an admission dean at one of the "top" Ivy League Colleges confided in me that only 25 percent of his class was admitted for strictly academic reasons.

Hence the commercialization of athletics, as it both confers preference in the college admission process and exaggerates the role of playing high school sports as an "investment" in the future, has exposed serious conflict between educational sensibilities and institutional self interest. How far can universities go in capitulating to commercial influences before they risk abdicating their public interest charge? This question invites educational leadership. It calls on college presidents to direct their athletic programs according to educational objectives, not in response to commercial cultural forces. It summons leadership that seeks to assert education's precious role in shaping culture.

Establishing the Right Perspective Regarding College Admissions

Harold Wingood
Dean of Admission, Clark University

"...collectively we have robbed America's students of their senior year."

Each fall, almost like clockwork, there is an explosion of activity in the media surrounding the college admissions process. It seems every commercial and public news organization does at least one story on the competitiveness of college admissions. In this frenzied environment, reporters and commentators talk primarily with the deans of admission at the most selective institutions in the country. They depict the process as being universally competitive, with every college and university rushing to deny admission to as many applicants as possible. This mania to be as selective as possible, they often opine, is driven by the pervasive rankings which they surmise have infected the admission decisions at most schools. This representation, however, does a great disservice to students, parents, and counselors because most colleges are not highly selective (and probably never will be), and most are unaffected by rankings. Yet that is not the story the media wants to tell.

In September 2001, James Fallows wrote an article—"Early-Decision Racket"—for *The Atlantic Monthly*, which fueled the perception that the only way to gain admission to a college or university was to apply as an early candidate. He went on to indict the process as being inherently unfair and a mechanism for colleges to drive down their acceptance rate and increase their yield. The topic quickly became the subject of television and radio talk shows, professional meetings of The College Board and the National Association for College Admission Counseling, and more. The overwhelming consensus was that Fallows was right, and that early decision programs unfairly give the advantage to students from private schools where the counseling tends to be more sophisticated and to children for whom financial aid is not a factor in their enrollment decisions. While there is some truth to this argument, it overstates the importance of the early process.

The release of Jacques Steinberg's *Gatekeepers*, the book in which a reporter details his experience at Wesleyan University as the staff proceeded through the admissions process, was this year's sensation. And again, it seemed that every news organization and talk show had to do a story about the topic of highly selective admissions. This phenomenon has been going on for years. There have been countless articles in the nation's newspapers and nearly as many books, from Michelle Hernandez's *A is for Admission* to Rachel Toor's *Admissions Confidential,* a book about the college admission process at Duke University. That they all sell like hotcakes and the national buzz they generate about going to college underscores our obsession with, and the media's exploitation of, a one-sided perspective of the subject. Regrettably, we end up doing a great disservice to the 1.3 million college bound students, their families, and counselors. The proclivity to present college admissions as impossibly difficult serves only to sell more newspapers and books, and does little to make the transition from high school to college a meaningful and educational extension of students' academic, intellectual, personal, and social development.

Spurred on by a relentless media barrage and sustained by many adults' inability to understand what is really important in the college-going process, collectively we have robbed America's students of their senior year. Their focus has shifted from enjoying the academic and co-curricular opportunities they have worked so hard to achieve, to scheming and even obsessing, about how to get into college. They no longer have the luxury of being high school seniors. Instead, they fixate on the December or April notification date as though that will define the quality of their four years in high school and validate them as individuals. It is almost as if all the hard work and dedication that preceded that last year had no meaning. Perhaps the most ludicrous part of it all is that the data is clear—the way the media is shaping our perspective about this critical life transition is simply wrong and misinformed, and very few voices have emerged to put the brakes on this runaway train.

Here then is the reality in which the media seems uninterested. For the vast majority of college bound American students, the process works, and it works well. According to data collected by Alexander Astin and his colleagues at UCLA's Cooperative Institutional Research Program (CIRP), which annually surveys thousands of first-year college students, the percentage of students who say they have enrolled in their first choice school has traditionally been over 70 percent. This year it fell to 69 percent, which may be a function of the increasing competition or average number of applications submitted per student, but the news is still quite good.

One also has to question the media's insistence on focusing on the nation's most selective institutions when, in fact, they serve a very small fraction of college bound students. In the fall of 2001, the last year for which there is data, *U.S. News & World Report* Best Colleges edition listed eighty-nine colleges and universities with an admit rate of 50 percent or less. Considering that there are roughly 2,500 accredited 4-year institutions of higher education in the United States, focusing, as the media does, on the most selective 4 percent presents a very warped sense of reality.

The same is true with the controversy regarding early decision. I remember James Fallows talking about early decision as though it were a pox on the college admissions process, and that the number of colleges and universities admitting 30 to 40 percent of their class through the early process was going to grow to the point where the average student would have severely limited options. Frankly, nothing could be further from the truth. The reality is that the vast majority of schools in the United States are unable to emulate the practices of the most visible and selective schools in the country. Of course, reporters like Fallows would not know that because they don't do reports on the 96 percent of the colleges and universities that are doing most of the heavy lifting in making sure our nation's most talented students are getting high quality educations.

The reality is that the vast majority of students in this country are not ready or able to commit early to a school. Among other things, financial aid considerations at most private institutions make it unwise. Additionally, students change during the course of their senior year and what may seem like a clear first choice in October may be a third choice in May when decisions are released. The bottom line in the debate is this: most schools that have early decision do well if they can enroll 10 percent of the class through such programs. If one were reading, watching, and listening to the media in fall 2001, one would have had to conclude that not having an early commitment in hand was tantamount to being left without a date on prom night. It is true that my colleagues in New England private secondary schools and affluent suburbs around Boston see a disturbingly high percentage of the class saying, "I want to go early, I just don't know where," and that piques the interest of the media, but the reality for most students headed for college is quite different.

So then, what is the best way to keep the college admissions process in its proper perspective? As with any major decision, be sure to look carefully beneath the surface. The major news organizations want us to fixate on that 4 percent of the schools that have far more qualified applicants than they can admit. They don't want college bound students and families to think about the schools like those described in Loren Pope's book, *Colleges That Change Lives*. While Loren's book is one of my personal favorites on the subject, it is just one of many that advise families to think critically about outcomes. Loren reminds us that one of the peculiar things about the United States is our tendency to evaluate the quality of a college by the profile of the enrolling students, not by what happens while students are enrolled.

The reality of college admissions is that most schools work very hard to recruit students who are a good fit. We care deeply about each student's capacity to take advantage of our faculty, facilities, relationship with fellow students, co-curricular programs, and setting. If one takes a look at the happiest and most successful individuals in the country, one quickly understands that no school has a corner on the market. The secret that the media works very hard to keep from the public's eye is this: the college-going process works very well for the vast majority of students in this country. Whether a student attends a school that admits 10 percent or 90 percent of the applicants, if the student and school are a good fit, then the chances that the student will move successfully and confidently on to the next stage of her or his career are excellent.

Students: You ARE Important, and You Can Take Control!

Matt Fissinger
Dean of Admission, Loyola Marymount University

"You are responsible for your education..."

Throughout this book, a variety of distinguished commentators have talked about the encroachment of commercialization on education. One dramatic result of the rise of commercial interests in education in general and college admission in particular is a feeling, on the part of those of you preparing to apply to college, that there are secrets you must buy to know, and rules dictated by external forces by which you must play in order to succeed. This understandably makes you feel that you have no control over this process, and we all feel terribly anxious about anything we do when the stakes are high and others are in control.

Wait! Don't panic—applying to college really isn't an alien experience! There are some good reasons that you can approach this journey with confidence that there will be more familiar terrain than you might initially expect.

Think about what you know about school, and about schools. Colleges and universities are, after all, just schools. Different kinds of schools, of course, but schools nonetheless. What are some of the characteristics you've observed in every school you've ever been associated with? What are some of the characteristics and ingredients which have made for good education?

First of all, the teachers are in charge, ultimately, at just about every school, and they will dictate the priorities and expectations for the community. How does this relate to your application? While the admission counselors who will be responsible for evaluating your application are not usually active teachers, they will be following policies which have almost undoubtedly been established by the university's faculty.

While teachers are in charge of schools, you are responsible for your education. If anything, this will be more true in college, where day-to-day "watchdogging" by teachers is replaced by an expectation that you are there to learn, that you care about learning, and that you will supply the curiosity and the discipline necessary to learn without the handholding and prodding of daily quizzes and assignments. In other words, you'll get the chance to focus on the challenge and excitement of learning, without always worrying about a series of prescribed hurdles and free from the insulation these externally imposed hurdles provide from the purest confrontations with uncomfortable and unfamiliar ideas.

Yet, you know what teachers always care about, and have always asked or required you to do, and this will not change: think clearly, organize your work carefully, write well, explore ideas with a thoughtful yet open mind, and don't be afraid to take some intellectual risks. They admire and reward ambition, and the ability to synthesize material into your own point of view. They help you understand that learning is a process, not a formula with an endpoint, and that using imagination and taking risks is how you really learn to learn.

These same values and skills apply to your college explorations and applications. You are, in the end, responsible for these, just as you are responsible for your education as a whole. Recognizing that familiar values and tools (imagination, discovery, growth, curiosity, writing, organization, and thoughtfulness) are applicable and valuable in applying to college, you may well find that the requirements of this process are not so alien after all, and that there's the prospect of a rewarding journey above and beyond merely "getting into school."

Three elements of the whole process often seem especially scary as you begin: finding the right college (out of the 3,000+ possibilities), organizing all the pieces and the details of your applications, and writing the dreaded essay—but these are pieces which most directly relate to the skills and experiences taught by teachers and practiced by students. Thus, you CAN approach them with confidence that you've tackled similar assignments and undertaken similar processes, or journeys of discovery, before. That kind of confidence—that you're in familiar territory—will allow you to develop a sense of control as you prepare and submit your applications. Let's look at each of these three elements:

Finding the right college

Think of finding the right college as a big research project. These are often the assignments we approach with the greatest apprehension, but they are often the ones which stimulate the most thinking and produce the greatest rewards. They seem overwhelming at first, and even though you begin with some sense of where you'll come out, you also know that the path you take and the questions you ask can lead to some unexpected results. You also know that you can't predetermine the answer, and that there's no good shortcut to finishing the project.

Researching colleges is more like a social science research project than hard science, because you'll be dealing with a human being— you! There's no absolutely precise way to measure your human abilities and shortcomings, and there's no way to predict what the relationship will be between the person you are today and who you'll become over the next several months and years. Social scientists must accept some ambiguity in their work, just as you must accept some ambiguity in your conclusions about college. Human unpredictability is a constant in social science research, in your exploration of colleges, and in education itself. Still, you can approach your work with confidence and excitement, because no one is better equipped to undertake the project or make use of the results than you.

You begin with a question: what type of college is right for you? You answer this through an objective review of the evidence and the data. In this case, you—your personality, your talents, your strengths, and your weaknesses—are the evidence. Objective measures of your performance and preparation—your grades and test scores and anything else you can use—provide the data. Good researchers approach data and evidence with scrupulous objectivity and genuine curiosity—what will I find? Where does this evidence and data point? While the hard work is all yours, experienced observers, including parents, friends, teachers, and counselors can help you interpret the evidence.

Your work on the evidence should lead you to a set of characteristics you seek in a college, including size, location, academic offerings, campus culture, selectivity, etc. Next, you gather more detailed information on a set of colleges presenting these characteristics. This is easy—we're all happy to tell you all about the colleges we represent.

Finally, you bring all your research skills to bear on these colleges. You read the literature, you interview the subjects (students at those colleges), you gather opinions from expert observers (friends, parents, alumni, etc.), and ask tough questions, especially of those whose objectivity you might find suspect (the Admissions Office). Your conclusions—the set of colleges to which you'll apply—are the result of synthesizing all the information you've gathered, and represent your judgment based on all the evidence.

Organizing your applications

This is a time management issue, and a project which requires great attention to detail. Certainly, these are skills your teachers and parents have encouraged you to practice throughout your life as a student.

Making sure you are aware of your deadlines, and giving yourself enough lead time are the keys. You will also need to be realistic about how long it will take to fulfill your responsibilities, and you'll need to be sensitive to the constraints facing those who will assist you in this process.

Just as your already busy life requires you to plan ahead, and just as you've become accustomed to coordinating complex schedules, you'll find that some clear and timely thinking about how you'll manage your applications will transform the mechanics of doing so from mysterious to predictable.

Get a calendar, or develop a timeline, then identify the deadlines and milestones, and work backwards from there to find your starting points. Ask your recommenders how much time they will need to prepare your letters, and find out from school when you'll need to request your transcripts in order for them to arrive on time. If you see a period where lots will be due all at once, either because several of your schools have similar deadlines or because important school assignments or other obligations overlap with your application period, give yourself extra lead time.

It all sounds simple, but in real life, these plans often slip. This is where another talent you've worked hard to develop comes in handy—discipline. With planning and discipline, you'll get all your applications organized and submitted on time, and it won't seem like anything out of the ordinary.

The essay

Well, what do you think you've been writing all these essays for, all throughout your school career? You've been in training for a moment just such as this, when your writing skills can make a difference, and help you achieve an important success.

There's nothing different expected of your college essay than is expected from every other writing assignment you've ever completed. Here's where those teachers come in again, both the ones who have taught you in high school, and the ones who await you in college. Your high school teachers have helped you prepare for this type of assignment, and the college teachers are waiting to assess your skills, too.

It doesn't matter what the topic is, or even how you answer the question. Your essay will be evaluated on how well it is conceived and written. So, remember your lessons. Organize your thoughts, present your ideas systematically, be careful to use proper grammar and correct spelling, and speak with your own voice. Don't try to figure out whether there's a correct answer—don't your teachers always encourage you to define and defend a point of view? The rules here are no different. The stakes may feel higher, and they are, but that's what you train for, like practicing for an important game. You know how to do this! Just put your skills to work, and trust yourself.

Conclusion

We all feel more confident in familiar territory than in unknown lands. We have a sense of control if we know the path we're following and the tools we'll need to reach our destination. Can we eliminate every uncertainty? Of course not, but what fun would that be? Eliminating uncertainty eliminates adventure and discovery. We still believe we'll get where we're going, and acknowledging uncertainty leaves us open to growth.

Applying to college is a unique and crucial transitional phase in your educational journey, but a piece of this whole experience called your education nevertheless. By breaking down the various requirements of applying to college, and applying the skills you know bring success in every other aspect of your educational life, you will gain a sense of familiarity, and a significant measure of control over this process.

Listening to What Matters

Craig J. Franz, FSC
President, St. Mary's College of California

"...the rankings are largely irrelevant to the student experience...avoid formulaic decision making...think for yourself."

As President of Saint Mary's College of California, a coeducational liberal arts college located in a suburban community twenty miles east of San Francisco, I'm sure my aspirations for St. Mary's are similar to those of many of my colleagues. I want my school to be known for its academic excellence. I want us to be known for the depth of our engagement in social issues, attentiveness to the needs of students, quality of athletic offerings, variety of extracurricular offerings, accessibility to the marginalized, and the diversity of our community.

I also want a favorable ranking for my school in the annual *U.S.News & World Report* rating of colleges and universities. Not because it accurately or meaningfully contrasts one institution to another—its empirical shortcomings are well known in academia—but because the publication is well marketed and widely consulted.

Each year, *U.S.News* uses a mathematical "formula" that takes numerous, differently weighted factors and aggregates them into a composite index score. Factors include how many alumni contribute annually to the institution; number of applicants; percentage of students accepted; average SAT score; and a totally subjective "reputation index." While any of these factors *may* reflect the integrity of an institution (more alumni contributions generate greater capital for operations, higher SAT scores mean enhanced intellectual firepower), they scarcely reflect what a student experiences at a particular institution. And, if the rankings are largely irrelevant to the student experience, what is their value?

Perhaps my concern is better expressed through a recent personal experience. While meandering around a Barnes & Noble bookstore, I spotted two high school seniors perusing the latest college rankings from *U.S.News*. I ambled over and talked with them about their aspirations for college. One desired a large urban (non-research) university with a strong football program and a solid engineering program. The other was interested in an education degree from a smaller rural college offering a Great Books curriculum. Despite such evidently divergent interests, they were examining schools rated in a single category for size and comprehensiveness of degree programs. Even more incredibly, after reviewing the ratings they were considering attending the *same school*.

Indeed, given the diversity of interests and aptitudes of high school seniors, it is hard to conceive of any mathematical formula that could transform raw data into a rating system offering meaningful (much less useful) comparative analysis. While I am doubtful that such a formula could exist, I am certain that the rating system employed by *U.S. News* doesn't do the job. (Of course, one wonders what will happen to *our* ratings once this book is published).

I am amazed at the avalanche of college annual reports, brochures and other print collateral that stack up on my desk each year during the spring. I'm not naive enough to think I'm special. It's simply that these institutions want to keep their name in front of me and the other 3,000+ college and university presidents across the United States polled annually by *U.S.News*. We are essentially asked to rank colleges against each other on the basis of "reputation." (Peer evaluations account for 25 percent of a college's rating in this survey.) Institutional familiarity portends higher ratings, so the public relations blitz continues year after year. One can only wonder if the cost to design and mail these increasingly sophisticated marketing pieces could be better invested in student learning.

Similarly, if our institution commits more money to admissions marketing, we surely can get greater coverage among prospective students. Heightened visibility is likely to increase our inquiry pool and very likely the number of applications (another variable used in the *U.S.News* rankings), thus giving us an edge against similar colleges. When faced with the decision to hire another tenured faculty member or make a bigger investment in marketing, I'd invariably elect to invest in students first and promotion second. The situation is further clouded when institutions are encouraged to have more and more students apply and pay the associated processing fee (hence boosting their selectivity and *U.S.News* rating) even though they have capped their enrollment and likely have no additional seats to offer to a broader pool of recruited students. It's no different than over-selling airplane seats—but the stakes are undeniably higher.

Another reason to question the value of one-size-fits-all college rankings: they imperil the rich diversity of higher education in America. Imagine a scenario in which every institution seeks the highest possible rating on up to fourteen different "quality" indices. As each institution gets closer to maximizing their performance on each of these variables, the institutions also become more homogenous. Over time, all institutions move towards the same target (a statistical phenomenon called "moving towards the mean") and start to look more and more alike. As a biologist, I know the environmental dangers inherent in the elimination of native wild stocks through the development of a predominant monoculture. As a college president, I fear a similar dissolution of the fertile, diverse, rich academic heterogeneity that has helped make American tertiary education the envy of the world.

While these popularity ratings should be viewed skeptically, another survey model now used by approximately 400 institutions deserves a closer look. The National Survey of Student Engagement (NSSE) is based less on predetermined calculations and more on experiential factors. Students—not administrators—are polled. Questions appear to be focused on the quality of learning and cultural environments. A serious attempt is made to evaluate the kinds of activities and resources students experience in their academic enterprise. The NSSE survey was crafted by thoughtful academicians to expose what's "behind the curtain" at our colleges and universities—something *U.S. News* and other popularized ratings, in my opinion, don't do very well. While legitimate to debate the value of any statistical instrument purporting to offer a single recommendation or ranking of one school in comparison to another, the NSSE survey is more informative than many. Ask if the school you're considering participates in NSSE and ask to see the latest results. They make for interesting reading.

So—if you can't rely on surveys to help map your educational future, what should you do? Put down the magazines and guides. Log off the Internet (those incessant pop-up ads must be annoying you, anyway). Spend time *talking* with people attending the schools you're considering. Ask them what they like and dislike about their school. Are the professors available after class hours? Are the classes taught by teaching assistants? What is the level of engagement between instructor and student during (and outside of) class? What is the campus like? Do professors ever involve students in research? How rigorous are the academics? Is creativity celebrated, or frowned upon? Do students willingly help one other with papers, tests, and seminars, or does it feel like they're in a fiercely competitive jungle? Nothing against competition, by the way—but undergraduate school needn't be cutthroat to be enriching.

Question anything that intrigues you. I once grilled an admissions officer about a yearbook picture I'd seen of a toilet paper dispenser with the words "Diplomas: take one" scribbled on the wall over the roll. I asked the admissions counselor if other students felt similarly. We got into a fabulous discussion about student creativity, intellectual freedom, lack of censorship, and the rights and responsibilities of student journalists. I got genuine insight into what that university was like. Four years later, I happily graduated from that institution. (And yes, I'm proud to display my *real* diploma.)

Students comparing two or more college options often feel they're stuck in a quagmire of data and abstract information. They are swamped with brochures, videos, web sites, printed materials, and forms. Oh, the forms! After the typical campus visit (formal tour, visits with admissions counselors and financial aid advisors, meetings with faculty from various academic disciplines, perhaps lunch in a dining hall) you can't help but feel overwhelmed. I once met a bright, engaging prospective student at the beginning of our "Open House" program. When I bumped into him at the end of a full day of speeches and activities, he looked exhausted. He was a victim of circuit overload. I felt sorry for him.

Colleges want you to know everything about them because, ultimately, they want the "fit" to be right. They would much rather have you as a student for four years than for only one. Students who transfer generally have little positive to say about the school they've just left. As a rule, negative opinions reach ten times more people than compliments. Look carefully at each school. Ask yourself it it's a place you can see yourself "being" for four or more years. If not, don't be afraid to remove it from your list of choices.

Once you have made your choice, you should be excited! Get yourself fully engaged into your new community. Take time to become acquainted with faculty, staff, and fellow students. Get involved in different activities that seem to interest you. Apply yourself rigorously to your class work, but *experience* your school. Your ultimate level of satisfaction with your choice of schools will be linked to your level of involvement with the community. The more you pour yourself into your college experience, the more you will cherish it.

The bottom line: Make an informed decision, taking into account your unique interests and abilities. Don't expect formulaic surveys to make the right choice for you.

Saving Imagination

Philip Ballinger, Ph.D.
Director of Admissions, University of Washington

*"Let us all—counselors, students and parents—reclaim the college
selection and admission process as a form of education rather than a
form of commercialism."*

I had a remarkable experience in Hawaii interviewing a prospective student. First of all, I interviewed the student, not the parents. This may not sound terribly remarkable, yet the reader must know that more often than not the parents of college-bound children take the lead. Sometimes it seems as if the parents are going to college with the child as an accessory. While I do not mind talking with parents about their children's college options or their very legitimate parental concerns, I am always heartened when a "child" shows a step towards independence and adulthood by taking the lead in the college selection process. This can be an educational process for young people and a foretaste of the initiative they will need to exercise in college.

In this instance, the student (let's call her Sarah) came to the interview on her own. I asked Sarah if her parents were coming in later and she said, "No—they feel that this is my decision and choice and that I need to take care of it." Concerned that Sarah may not have had sufficient parental support for her college aspirations, I asked whether or not her parents were involved in her college selection and application process. She assured me that they were involved, but mostly through asking her what she was learning about schools and by telling her what they could afford. She then went on to share with me that her mother continually asked questions not about college but more about Sarah herself. Questions such as, "What do you want college to be like?" "What do you want college to feel like?" "What are the students like?" "What do you want to do in college?" "What would be perfect? Describe it to me." "What is most important to you in college?" I must admit, this was one interview in which I truly wanted to meet the parent if only to applaud her—she was supporting Sarah by turning her inwards, by nudging her towards her own imagination and, therefore, towards her as yet unspoken expectations, hopes, and dreams.

The results of this process for Sarah were remarkable. She was (and is) a superb student. She ended up having choices between two of the most selective institutions in the country as well as my own institution at the time—a moderately selective and esteemed school but certainly not a school with designer label cachet. Yet, during the college selection process, during her own measuring of heart through imagination, Sarah was able to share with me precisely what she hoped for in college and why she felt my institution could be a primary option. She was able to ask questions which flowed calmly from the "imagination work" she had done before meeting with me. Sarah arrived at good "knowledge" via working with her imagination. She came to a college decision that, in my opinion, flowed from both her being and mind, and it was a decision she made with some degree of peace. I find this remarkable because the college search and decision process today often has little to do with who a student is or what a student hopes for, but rather pre-empts, stresses, forces, allures, and confuses. Frankly, for many students, imagination and peace have little place in this maelstrom. Yet Sarah and others show me that selecting a college can be a good and completely human process still.

Whenever I infer something about the nature of humanity, I turn to philosophy by habit. In the philosophy of Immanuel Kant, the two fountains of human knowledge are intuition and understanding. The bridge between these two vital faculties is, for Kant, imagination. As Matthew E. Pacholec of Grinnell College notes, "Imagination is the indispensable hinge between intuition and understanding...the synthetic, synoptic character of knowledge could not be realized were it not for...imagination."[1] In poetic language, we could say with Gerard Manley Hopkins that imagination is "the fine delight that fathers thought."[2] In either case, whether philosophically or poetically worded, the essential nature of imagination in human life is clear—it leads to knowledge and it gives rise to intention and action. This is particularly true for the college selection process. Imagination should be the energy and the current moving a student's decision process. The ideal result of this process should be a decision that is confident, self-expressive, and, dare I say it, peaceful.

Navigating the college selection and admission process gives rise to the first major life decision for most seventeen- to eighteen-year-olds. It can be a self- defining process and an educational process—a process that should be honored and supported. Throughout fifteen years of admission experience, I have always taken joy in students who have delved into their imaginations. They took the time and they received the support they needed to assess their minds, their feelings, and their hopes through imagination. Unfortunately, I do not believe that much of the current culture surrounding the college selection and admission process supports the vital and wonderfully human power of imagination.

When I started in admission work, the weathered dean who hired me shared his expectations. "You are a counselor and teacher," he told me. "Your job is to assist students and families in making an important choice." He helped me see that admission counseling was worthy work and part of an institution's mission of education. Over the years I have noticed a sharp shift away from the model of counseling and teaching to one of marketing and "closing the deal." Everything has been "businessfied" much less commercialized. I cannot remember the last time I heard a college president, for example, talk about college admissions in terms of counseling and education (save in this book). Manipulation of choice has apparently become the art du jour and feeding off the resulting stress in students and their families has become the latest market of opportunity. Students and their families respond in kind. Their task in this context also becomes one of manipulation. In their case, they attempt to manipulate admission decisions and financial aid packages. Parents do this for the apparent good of their child, but what is lost in the midst of this maelstrom is the idea that college is about education and formation. I admit still being shocked by the lacunae that exist between admission processes and cultures, amid institutional missions at many colleges of note. Frankly, at some institutions, admission counselors should be called sales representatives, and directors of admission should be called sales managers. This would be honesty in labeling.

In the Jesuit tradition of formation and education, the concept of discernment is key. Discernment is a matter of choosing among alternatives. In this process of choice, the discerner uses his or her imagination to visualize possibilities and to "feel" what they are like. This is generally done in the context of meditation and often with the help of an advisor or counselor. The end result is that the discerner determines which choice offers an abiding sense of peace as opposed to disquiet. Imagination is the engine for this "node of discernment." I believe this can be true for "discerning" a college choice as well.

If we claim that the process of choosing a college is at heart an educational process, and if we further claim that this educational process concerns learning how to make important life choices well, then we should be concerned about the "de-educational" miasma surrounding this process. Education as a process of development of the human person has little to do with rankings, commercialism, and false precision. It has everything to do with imagination. Imagination is imprecise—it involves such vague realities as wonder, discovering the unknown, intuition, applying understanding, and moving towards action. The college selection process, as an educational process, has very little to do with the culture of "buying a product." Education is not a commodity. Choosing a college is not the same as choosing a tube of toothpaste. This should be self-evident, but apparently it is not.

Pedro Arrupe, a former Superior General of the Jesuits, wrote, "What seizes your imagination will affect everything! It will decide what will get you out of bed in the morning, what you do with your evenings, how you spend your weekends, what you read, who you know, what breaks your heart, and what amazes you with joy and gratitude." Imagination can play the same role in the college selection process. We must encourage and help our young people imagine college before choosing a college

A young person going to a college that has seized his or her imagination is off to a great start. How can we engage imagination in the college selection process? Here are some suggestions:

Start at the beginning

Why start with rankings, particularly when those rankings are driven by commercial concerns? Why start with conclusions drawn from criteria that may or may not be of importance for a particular child? Why not start with the child? My story about Sarah is a story about starting from the beginning: Sarah certainly researched colleges and gathered all sorts of information. She certainly spoke with all sorts of experts, both on the high school and college level. She certainly was active in attaining information about financial aid and scholarships. However, before she did all these things, she had already engaged in "imagining" college. Her mother helped her do this by asking foundational questions that nudged Sarah towards her own imagination. This in turn helped Sarah arrive at the general hopes and expectations she had concerning college. Sarah began to give voice to the hopes and expectations most important to her, and these led her to useful knowledge when she began her focused search. This "voice of imagination" helped her navigate the selection process and arrive at a decision truly her own and therefore truly engaging.

Make some room for quiet reflection and visualization

Both parents and students can take time to reflect and visualize. Time aside, time out, time within is not wasteful in the college selection process. It can be energizing. For parents, this time is a matter of imagining, visualizing, and *making explicit* in their own minds what they wish for their child. What do they hope for in the *most* foundational sense? Is hoping that Johnny or Mary gets into Harvard foundational, or is there something more primary behind this desire? Trying to separate their own needs and hopes from their child's needs and hopes in this process could prove helpful and practical. Boomer parents are amazingly influential upon their millennial children. Their sons and daughters are very observant and sensitive to the leads and signals parents send. If parents approach this decision as an educational process, their children may respond well and learn an important life lesson about decision making. Parents do well by asking first what they want for their child before asking themselves what college they want for their child.

Students particularly need quiet time, time for imagination, time to give word to their hopes and expectations regarding college. Sarah in Hawaii took this time, and her mother supported her by addressing Sarah's imagination. Her mother helped Sarah engage her heart, will, and intellect before she entered the commercialized storm surrounding college selection and entrance. Encouraging young people to "waste some time" in quiet thinking about college and imagining being in college is a marvelous thing to do. Giving them permission to do this before pushing them to "do" things is a kind of gift. Young people do have hopes and expectations regarding college. They know it is an opportunity to begin a new book of life if they wish to make changes, to grow, to become more. Imagination can help them draw outlines for these hopes and expectations which they can then apply to all the data and all the spin they will encounter.

Let us all—counselors, parents, and students—reclaim the college selection and admission process as a form of education rather than a form of commercialism. Let us turn our young people first to their imaginations, not towards market driven illusion and false precision. Let us relate to our young people as educators, not as sales persons. Let us help them to be students more than consumers as they approach college selection and entrance.

1 Mathew E. Pacholec, "Kant on the Imagination and Delirium," a paper presented at the Colloquium of the Association for Phenomenology and the Cognitive Sciences (London Richmond University, 2002).

2 Gerard Manley Hopkins, Poems and Prose, ed. by W.H. Gardner (London. Penguin Books, 1963). p. 68.

Summary and Discussion:
Seeking Educational Clarity and Inspiration

"Nobody likes what's going on in college admissions—not students, not parents, not college presidents and not deans."
Lee Pelton, President of Willamette University

The impulse propelling readers through these essays may well be the same impulse that inspired and brought the essays together. Something is wrong with college admissions—something wrong enough to care about, to discuss, and to change. While the concerns about commercialism's influence in college admissions vary in scope, they have become collectively compelling. And so we ask: Is there a conscience emerging from these concerns? What does it say? To whom does it speak? How can we each contribute to a more educationally responsible admissions environment? How can we work to reclaim studenthood from commercial intrusions?

The essayists, most of whom selected their own issues to address, are college presidents, seasoned admission veterans, counselors, and educators. All have witnessed and experienced the changes in college admissions wrought by commercialism—changes in practices, policies, attitudes, and behaviors among students, parents, counselors, and university officials. Their perspectives and particular interests vary, at times predictably so. But the range of opinions provides significant overlap from which to discern consensus.

In some ways, this book can be seen as an experiment in community expression for college admissions: a sort of neighborhood meeting—the kind that might naturally develop in response to threats or infringements on the shared values of the community. The attendance at this "meeting," the issues discussed, the passions expressed, the values revealed, and the suggestions made—all underscore the importance of this experiment as an expression of the educational character, health, and ambition of the college admission community.

Andrew Delbanco, a keenly qualified social critic, suggests that the history of American higher education can be seen as an ongoing struggle between two often conflicting obligations: a commitment to the moral development of a future citizenry inherited from our first universities' founders and churches, and an obligation to train a new generation of productive contributors to the economy. He wrote, "We want our institutions both to preserve our culture as we pass it on to our children and to prepare them for the task of revising and changing it. These dual functions are very difficult, if not impossible, to keep in balance." Today, the growing influences of institutional pressures and commercialized admission practices indicate a dangerous shift in this balance. "I can feel the balance shifting," adds Delbanco. "I find myself asking: How far can we go in protecting the bottom line before the institution we are protecting loses its soul?" The essayists in this book echo Delbanco's concern with balance as they also fear commercialism's undue influence in college admissions (*The College Board Review,* July, 1997*).*

The Problem—the commercially distorted marketplace of college admissions

What is the profile of the new student-unfriendly marketplace of college admissions? It is a landscape characterized by:

- The growing impact of "the ranksters" on nearly every aspect of college admissions.

- The "marketeering" of education through increased use of market concepts and strategies to package, position, price, and promote college education.

- The undue influence of outside agencies in selling colleges and students.

- The radical shift in the use of financial aid from helping needy students gain access to education to serving strategic institutional priorities in the marketplace of college admissions.

- The blatant "customerization" of students.

- The marketing of prestige, popularity, comfort, status, and brand as important educational criteria.

- The emulation of corporate behavior in the conduct of admission activities.

- The commercialization of student data.

- The growth of anxiety-selling by industries such as test prep, scholarship search, and athletic agents.

- The re-distribution of vast resources from investment in education to marketing.

- The dangerous rise in stress and stress-related illnesses among students involved in the college admission process.

- For students, the reduction in time committed to self-directed explorations of curiosity, thinking, and spending unstructured time with family and friends.

- For students, the obsession with strategizing versus experiencing while high school is increasingly seen as merely an audition for college.

- The increased reliance on tactics and gamesmanship in trying to be selective and in trying to be selected.

- The enhanced advantage given those who can afford to play the game.

- The troubling evaporation of ethical standards and the rise in blatant lies and falsification by colleges, students, and parents.

- The increasing "corporatization" of The College Board as it expands its influence and power in college admissions and K-12 education.

- The growing imbalance among college-going populations as defined by family income level.

- The out-of-control parents who increasingly try to "manage" their children's educational destinies.

- The rising obsession with quantification and false precision that skews everything from the college search process to measures of institutional quality, to benchmarks of success, and to the nature of learning and decision making.

- The exaggerated "tiering" of colleges—a clustering of high incomes, high test scores, fortunate kids, and excessive interest in a small group of colleges.

These have become the prominent commercial landmarks in contemporary college admissions. Yet, these are certainly not characteristics that conscientious educators would include in a model for higher education. Michael McPherson of The Spencer Foundation tells a story about a delegation of Swedish educators visiting America to study higher education. During dinner on the final night of their tour, the leader of the delegation remarked, "We have only one question: Who is in charge?"

And so confusion and concern reign, not only about who is in charge, but also about the values being expressed and served by a commercially- dominated college admissions marketplace. Inspired by the prospect of reshaping college admissions, our essayists bring educational discernment to this confounding public arena.

Seeking Educational Clarity—personal revelations

"Today's cutthroat competition in college admissions has less to do with real educational value than with a market-driven scramble for perceived value in an academic world where the difference between reality and perception is breaking down."
Andrew Delbanco, *New York Times Book Review,* September 29, 2002

"Still, there is something inherently attractive about trying to rate schools based on their selectivity. Such a rating seems to provide clarity. But the clarity is an illusion."
Don Peck, *The Atlantic Monthly*, November 2003

The conflict between commercial influences and educational values often reveals itself with clarifying, if not sobering effects. In the first essay, Kim Stafford writes with the combined sensitivity of being a parent, poet, and educator. He describes watching his daughter being courted by college admission representatives, and how the tactics and language used defy his own educational sensibilities. "I want someone to be loyal to the drama of her journey," a journey down the "path of not knowing—yet—for this is what college is for." And, what matters most in this journey he recognizes is, "what the student brings, this is the treasure...some power that is in you now will help you then [when you go to college]."

Similarly illuminating examples of educational clarity have been described by many of the essayists. Bill Shain binds his essay between two inspiring quotes—one from a song, the other from a comic strip. Both shape his message that grown-ups are at fault for the distortion of college admissions, that grown-ups have a responsibility to be ethical role models, that these grown-ups include parents, reporters, admission officers, and high school counselors. "All of us would be well advised to heed (the advice): 'We have met the enemy, and they is us.'"

The collision between educational and commercial values struck Ted O'Neill during a posh party hosted by The College Board atop the World Trade Center. While circulating at the party, he sensed a change: "A new team had come on, and their style was different." Trying to explain this observation, he suggests that all educators share some things in common, but these commonalities now seem alien to the new team at The College Board. "The bottom line [for educators] is different, and has to do with learning, not profit and not power," he writes. Long a member of The College Board, Ted laments, "...at that point I began to feel like someone along for the ride, not a member, not one of the people at the forum."

Michael Beseda, Philip Ballinger, and Robert Massa all describe experiences they had with students as being instrumental in helping clarify and convey their messages in this book. The four words, "I want to learn," submitted as a college essay many years ago, continue to remind Beseda that learning is becoming increasingly de-emphasized "in the commercialized world of college admissions…" By comparison, today's college essays seem so contrived and full of strategizing. Similarly, Ballinger worries that the commercial messages inundating students prevent them from approaching college selection with a healthy and receptive imagination. Robert Massa credits plenty of his admission wisdom to watching his own children survive the college admission onslaught. "Look, Dad," Massa reports his son saying in response to Dad's badgering, "if a college is not going to admit me because I took honors physics as a senior rather than as a junior, I don't want to go to that college."

The examples cited above suggest that among the essayists (and most admission professionals, I believe), there is an impulse to understand and serve the educational needs of students—an impulse which is often revealed through personal experiences. This impulse has drawn many people to the field of college admissions and accounts for the rising outrage against commercialization. These professionals share basic instincts about what makes education special and, therefore, necessarily off-limits to commercial influences. In a culture so dominated by marketing, admission professionals must often rely on the light of these educational instincts while steering through the cynical shadows cast by commercial influences.

Seeking Educational Clarity—articulating judgments

Beyond mere impulse and instinct, there exist common threads of understanding that propel our essayists in seeking educational clarity. The essayists agree that certain norms or values are necessarily attached to education—norms and values which make education off-limits to commercial intrusions. Through the use of declarations such as "should," "should not," "that is not the way," and "it is immoral," the essayists express reactions to commercialism beyond mere impulse. They are articulating judgments about commercialism based on an understanding of educational values, the importance of those values, and the role of college admissions in serving those values.

Massa comments on the misplaced importance of status: "What a terrible way to pursue a higher education, and what a misguided definition of success we have developed as a society." Mark Speyer is concerned with the cumulative impact of various commercial influences on student learning: "…we do have a problem on our hands. We are torturing our young people, and sending them less prepared to college than they were ten years ago." Harold Wingood is critical of media distortion: "…the way the media is shaping our perspective about this critical life transition is simply wrong and misinformed, and very few voices have emerged to put the brakes on this runaway train." Ted O'Neill worries about the impact of standardized testing on basic social organization: "Imposing exams means imposing a curriculum…. The more we institutionalize exam results as the measure of intelligence, diligence, and worth of a child (and the value of teachers and schools and communities), the more we invite the creation of hierarchy in America…." And Karl Furstenberg blames several sources for "making students and families unnecessarily anxious" by "focusing too much attention on the admission process."

Our college presidents are also issuing warnings. "Far too many college students choose their colleges for all the wrong reasons.…It doesn't have to be that way.…You don't have to play their game," writes Richard Hersh. William Adams urges his colleagues: "Complicity (with *U.S.News*) is a disservice to our students and prospective students, and it helps distort various public policy issues affecting higher education." Colin Diver warns: "…the emphasis on instrumental values has gone so far as to create the impression that there is no place in higher education for those who care about pursuing knowledge for its own sake."

And Craig Franz cautions that the rankings are not only "irrelevant to the student experience," but they "imperil the rich diversity of higher education in America...as institutions move towards the same target."

Capitulation by colleges and universities to commercial influences is an important part of the problem. "Colleges have become exceptionally brilliant, if unintentionally, in their creation of a market frenzy...," proclaims Bruce Poch. Paul Marthers admits that admission professionals "can seem like masters of the bait and switch." Michael Beseda points out that "it is really no wonder that we are identified in this way [as a sales force] by those in and outside of academe." Phil Ballinger describes a troubling shift in the admission profession: from counseling to sales. He declares, "at some institutions, admission counselors should be called sales representatives, and directors of admission should be called sales managers." This almost clarion call comes from Jim Sumner: "...the vast inaccuracy of that data (submitted to various publishers by colleges) leads prospective students, their families, and school counselors/advisors far astray each year....What I wish for is abandonment of the blatant falsification of data...." Finally, we hear from a strident Sean Callaway: "The purpose of education is lost to prestige in the ranking recruitment wars....When post-secondary educational corporations, building on parental, high school, and peer pressure, knowingly induce fear and emotional stress to create a sellers' market and drive the supply of applicant characteristics, it's immoral. While it may make business sense to use every tool of predictive modeling, one-to-one marketing, and sophisticated emotional market manipulation to increase yield, from the point of view of fostering the growth of adolescents' cognitive and affective maturity, it's cannibalism."

Emerging from these value-laden statements is a common and convincing perception: commercial influences are having educationally inappropriate consequences. More and more educators are realizing that commercially-prescribed practices are violating and distorting educational norms.

Seeking Educational Clarity—a group exercise

During a recent conference of The National Association for College Admission Counseling, approximately 200 admission professionals participated in a group exercise that dramatically revealed the disconnect between commercial admission practices and educational values. The group was first asked to identify why they had selected college admissions as a profession. Most agreed that working with students was a primary motivator. Asked to identify what it was that made students so attractive, the group identified the following "student characteristics": curiosity, innocence, energy, intellectual risk taking, creativity, humility, independent thinking, willingness to take risks, imagination, courage, interest in doing the right thing, compassion, and an interest beyond self—a desire to make a difference in the community. These student qualities inspire many admission officers, and passion for these qualities was quite obvious during this part of the exercise.

Next, this group of admission professionals described their institutional mission statements. It quickly became apparent that college mission statements are fairly similar. Most colleges seek to prepare students to lead both meaningful and productive lives. They extol the value of liberal arts education in fostering critical thinking, citizenship, leadership, moral judgment, flexibility, civic mindedness, big picture thinking, creativity, tolerance for ambiguity, and the ability to take the long look undisturbed by self interest and prejudice. Participants eagerly contributed to this discussion, as if celebrating with colleagues from other colleges their common sense of professional identity.

Having quickly identified the student qualities that inspire these professionals and the complementary institutional goals that encourage them to foster these qualities, the delighted group was asked to examine the practices that characterize contemporary college admissions. Suddenly, the mood in the room grew pensive. After an initial round of quiet seat squirming and prompts from the moderator, responses began to emerge with increasing frequency and alarm. There began a general discussion of the commercial influences, including some of the "commercial landmarks" mentioned earlier. But, as examples of specific admission practices were offered (at times reluctantly), an obvious and growing sense of disturbance supplanted the mood of professional camaraderie. A high school counselor in the group described an advertisement in *The New York Times Magazine* for an Ivy League college's summer school program: "The courses last five weeks, the bragging rights last forever." Another counselor recalled the various letters from admission deans with remarkably similar messages which he paraphrased: "It was another record year in admissions as we received 10 percent more applications...." Then there were recollections of phrases used by admission representatives in front of prospective students, including: "We have the best faculty in your area of study," "Our drama program is second to none," "The difference between our students and those at other colleges is the passion they have in the classroom." Many stories began to emerge, some from admission officers, most from high school counselors. These stories included the solicitation of names of high school juniors by colleges, the direct mail recruitment of juniors encouraging them to finish high school while attending college, promises of better scholarship possibilities for early applicants, waiting lists longer than admit lists, counseling students to take the SAT as many times as possible, the packaging and selling of SAT test prep services by a popular college, and a college using its rank to advertise itself while at the same time discounting the value of rank. During this part of the session, tensions seemed to rise between college officials and high school counselors.

In closing, the moderator summarized and compared the conclusions from each part of the session. First, he recounted the all-important and inspiring student characteristics which root admission colleagues in this personally rewarding educational profession. Then he repeated the professional and institutional goals which unite these colleagues under a high calling to serve the student characteristics. Finally, he offered a picture of the commercial admissions landscape, providing a discomforting juxtaposition between values and practices, and begging the final question: "How can we expect anything less from ourselves than we do from our students?"

Reclaiming Studenthood—advocating educational values

"The college admission process should be different from all other rational consumer assessments. There is no unbiased measure of the quality, reliability, and dependability of colleges, and we are irresponsible to act like there is."
Lee Bollinger, College Board Forum keynote address, January 31, 2002

The current crisis in college admissions reflects a troubling disconnect between educational purposes and market-driven practices. In a society whose culture is increasingly being determined and defined by private-sector commercial norms, educational leaders have a unique obligation to resist inappropriate commercial influences and to defend and champion the unique role of higher education in shaping our culture. Unfortunately, in college admissions, it seems we have lost sight of that calling. While we can feel and fear the disconnect, we too often seem immobilized in pursuing education's call.

"An example of social waste that I think rivals the SUV…," writes Swarthmore College Professor, Barry Schwartz, describing the "arms race" for elite students among elite colleges ("Tyranny of Choice," *The Chronicle of Higher Education*, January 23, 2004). As part of the "shopping mall" arsenal of tactics employed by colleges and universities to lure students as customers, "obsession with choice" has had demonstrably negative impacts on students, including debilitating levels of fear and anxiety. This obsession, according to Schwartz, constitutes an "abdication of responsibility by university faculty and administrators." He encourages more responsible behavior by institutions that have been overly influenced by "principles and practices of neoclassical economics."

Choice is not the only questionable commercial concept in the confounding market place of college admissions. Our essayists have expressed similar concerns about the educational appropriateness of competition, rationality, product, brand, consumer primacy, "more is better," "perfect fit," market value, self-interest, etc. Relevant questions about the appropriateness of these commercial concepts include: How can students and colleges be expected to act with consumer certainty during selection processes that are necessarily filled with so many important unmeasurables? If learning is about growth discovery and change, how can students be asked to make decisions with such exactitude as implied by selection of "the perfect college"? Is competition that creates winners and losers, according to criteria defined by agencies outside of education, acceptable? To what extent are processes that reward gamesmanship by the wealthy educationally justifiable? Is brand a guarantee of quality education? If we cannot measure and compare and promote certain qualities, are they then not important? Should we manage and shape educational institutions according to commercially defined criteria? Does prestige confer value? To what extent can and should educational values and value be relegated to market mechanisms? If we expect students to be honest, visionary, and civic-minded, how can we expect anything less of ourselves?

Thinking about these questions in the context of the essays, we can expand the "The Tyranny of Choice" theme to a more encompassing "The Tyranny of brand, of rank, of score, of more is better, of the one perfect school, of prestige, of student as customer, of playing the game, of being a salesperson, of education as product, of more is better, of winning at any cost, etc." The focus and weight of the essays confirm that there is a crisis in college admissions—a disconnect between educational purposes and commercial practices. For there be change, colleges must acknowledge the role they have played in turning college admissions into a marketplace, and move from being part of the problem to being part of the solution. But there seem to be hurdles.

More than twenty-five years ago, B. Alden Thresher, an economist-turned-college-admission-dean, wrote a seminal essay about college admissions and the public interest. Thresher argued that in order to serve the greater societal purposes of education, college admission deans needed to recognize their own institutional self-interests and rise above them. Recently, Mike McPherson and Morton Schapiro, also economists, wrote that although colleges were educationally uncomfortable with the increasing use of financial aid as a "competitive weapon," "most colleges and universities have very little ability to influence this situation by their individual actions" (*The Student Aid Game*). Today the voices in this collection of essays express a collective affirmation to serve educational obligations amid disrupting commercial influences. Ours is a new campaign for studenthood.

The use of the term "studenthood" is strategic. It is an enveloping, summary idea. It is a creative attempt to appeal to educational sensitivities and sensibilities. It offers the hope of a socially responsible alternative to inappropriately invasive market-driven rationality. For if we care about education, we should be fundamentally committed to serving the educational needs of students. And if we are to help young people become good students, then we should value and understand what it means to be a student. Finally, if what we value and care about is being threatened, then we must act with appropriate conservator's zeal.

Studenthood, again, refers to those qualities which define and give value to being a student—things such as curiosity, imagination, confidence, effort, compassion, and sense of wonder. It includes the student attitude and willingness to engage these qualities in the activity of learning. These qualities make learning happen, they make learning special, they establish the student at the strategic center of education. Accordingly, by recognizing and celebrating studenthood as a resource, college admission participants can develop commensurate educational values or principles by which to establish appropriate admission practices.

Examples of such principles were identified by the Advisory Board of the Education Conservancy:

- Education is a process, not a product. Students are learners, not customers.

- The benefits and predictors of good education are knowable, yet virtually impossible to measure.

- Rankings oversimplify and mislead.

- A student's intellectual skills and attitude about learning are more important than where that student goes to college.

- Educational values are best served by admission practices that are consistent with these values.

- College admissions should be part of an educational process directed toward student autonomy and intellectual maturity.

- Colleges can be assessed but not ranked. Students can be evaluated but not measured.

- Students' thoughts, ideas, and passions are worthy to be engaged and handled with utmost care.

These principles may be discounted by critics for being overly simplistic and obvious. However, what is even more obvious is the contradiction between these principles and the commercial practices and conditions which have come to characterize and influence contemporary college admissions. What is simple to recognize is that expressed educational values and purposes (including honesty) are being disserved, if not violated, by those entrusted with their stewardship. If we are to realign college admissions practices with educational purposes, we can begin by committing ourselves to these principles in a way that is compelling. As Andrew Delbanco so ironically suggests, "We must find a way to lend prestige to a change in policy" (The College Board Forum keynote address, January 18, 2002). In fact, we can and must find ways to celebrate these essential educational principles—principles that have been all but sacrificed to commercial expedience.

Recommendations: Who can do what needs to be done?

All inhabitants of the college admissions community have a role to play in resisting the commercialization of college admissions—all have opportunities for educational pay-off. Parents, students, counselors, admission deans, college presidents, even The College Board and the media—all can contribute to the educational health of college admissions. Appropriate actions can be derived from a commitment to genuine educational goals, from an appreciation of studenthood. Accordingly, the following recommendations are offered to help re-establish college admissions as a student-centered, educationally responsible process.

What can students do?

Read the essays in this book! Where else will you find four hundred years of collective experience aimed at helping you make the most of your college admission process? These essays were written out of concern for students by people whose lives have been dedicated to serving the same. Expertise, insight, compassion, and advice are all here for your benefit. Read and learn how to celebrate your studenthood.

In your reading, you will notice some educationally nutritious themes emerging. Digest these slowly and thoroughly, and govern yourself according to their richly fortifying content. You will be a stronger, wiser, and more effective applicant as a result.

Theme One: College is what you make of it. Your need for learning, your desire to know, your appetite for new activities and new ideas; your willingness to be stretched beyond your comfort zone; your tolerance for ambiguity; your fondness for hard work; your interest in people, places and things; and your passion for life—these are your educational assets. These are what you must invest if you want to make (not get) "a good college education."

No particular college can provide the benefits that you are responsible for generating by using your own educational assets.

Theme Two: Confidence counts. Since you are in charge of making education happen, you might want to learn a bit about yourself. Don't fret, you can't know everything—that is why you are going to college: to learn! But you might try taking inventory of your educational assets by considering those mentioned above and talking with your friends, teachers, and even your parents about how rich you are in each area. While you are doing this, allow yourself to think about education and your experiences as a student. What have been your rewards and your struggles? What makes learning different from all other activities? What do you like and dislike about learning? Do you have favorite teachers and subjects? What makes these favorites? If you could change anything about your high school, what would it be and why? What do you wonder about? If you had a year to do whatever you wanted, what would you do? Do you learn best when you are comfortable; or when you are stretched, challenged or confronted with foreign ideas? After considering these questions, look through a college's catalog and see which of the course descriptions sound interesting. Use your imagination. Be true to the student you have become. Trust your instincts and educational impulses. Be curious about what you do not know, not fearful about the impact of not knowing. Allow uncertainty to inspire you. Confidence counts.

Theme Three: You are doing precision guesswork, nothing more—and that is OK. You cannot possibly know all there is to know about any college. No one can. And you cannot know all there is to know about yourself. Remember that you are a student. Relax, take a deep breath, and believe in yourself.

Theme Four: There is no such thing as the one perfect college. Yes, there are many colleges from which to choose, but that does not mean there is one perfect or even one best choice. There are many more similarities among colleges than there are meaningful differences! While colleges can be grouped according to certain common characteristics, such as size, liberal arts vs.

research orientation, location, cost, religious affiliation, special programs and majors, personality, etc., it should not be too tough to identify those characteristics which seem to be suitable for you. You should then be able to put together a group of colleges that are similar enough that any one of them will suit your educational assets. More than 80 percent of students report getting into their "first choice college." And many more report that after a year, their college has become their first choice college. They have made it that way.

Theme Five: Resist the marketplace mentality of college admissions. Think about the following: Is education a product? Is the student a consumer? Do rank, brand, reputation, and status have much to do with educational quality? Does where you go to college have much to do with how much money you will make in the future—and how important is that? As you do your reading, you will come to know the answers to these questions. Therefore, be skeptical of all educational sales pitches which ignore your studenthood. Recognize that when it comes to education, "you are not the 'customer' and you are not 'always right'," according to Richard Hersh. In fact, making mistakes and turning those mistakes into learning experiences is a hugely educational experience. Therefore, do not be afraid to say, "I do not know what my perfect college is," and "I don't know what I want to major in," and "I like both big classes and small classes," and "I don't know what it means to be a college student, yet. These are all things I look forward to discovering when I get to college. But I have hunches, and I will trust them. Let me claim my right to make my own decisions about education, let me exercise being a student."

Theme Six: There will always be exceptions. In other words, some of these themes may not apply to your particular situation or values. For example, you may know exactly what you want to major in. (By the way, something like 90 percent of students change their majors at least once during college). Or you may want to pursue a special activity, such as a sport, in college. (By the way, most students who begin playing a sport in college do not end up playing for four years. That is because they realize how many other things there are to do in college.) Or you may simply believe that some of the themes just don't suit your situation and family values. That is OK. What is most important is the amount of control you exert in this college planning process; the more you are in control, the better the educational outcome will be.

Beyond these themes for developing a better approach to college admissions, some students always ask for specific, strategic suggestions.

Consider the following:

- Resist taking any standardized test more than twice.

- Are you applying to a college just because the application process is easy?

- Do you want to put something as important as your heart in the hands of an admission dean?

- Should you let an admission dean, test score, GPA, or coach tell you what you are worth?

- Carefully consider your reasons for accepting a position on any college's waiting list, and make sure you are set to go to a college to which you have been admitted. If you have selected your colleges confidently, you should have options.

- Should you view your high school experience as merely a training run for college, during which everything you do becomes an effort to appease the college admission gods?

- Try to limit the number of college applications you submit to no more than four to six. Studies show that students who apply to fewer colleges, once they have done reasonable research, often have better rates of acceptance and college success.

- Approach high school as a necessary, significant, and enjoyable part of your life.

- Make high school count by identifying and exploring your curiosities and passions.

- Take appropriately challenging courses; you are in charge of deciding what is appropriate.

- Limit the amount of time you spend in front of the television.

- Allow yourself to enjoy down time, spontaneity, and unstructured play. Your generation has been described as the most plugged in but least connected; let yourself go unplugged for a while.

- Remember: The more popular the college, the more political the admission process and the less control you have in that process.

- Keep in mind that you are being judged according to criteria that you would never use to judge another person and which will never again be applied to you once you leave college.

- Consider taking a year off between high school and college to work or follow your passions.

Finally, for those times when anxiety and pressure about college admissions become overwhelming, when you feel confused and unsure and out of steam, when the impulse to scream "College, go away!!!" seems to be your only option....During these moments of uncertainty, try reciting the following lines as a kind of student cheer, as a way of reminding yourself of your own importance in a process which does not have to be so brutal. Here is a way to celebrate your studenthood. Here is your student mantra. Exclaim:

YES, the anxiety I feel about the college admissions process is not necessary; and

YES, my frustration about being treated as a consumer all my life only to have a numbing dose heaped on me by the college admissions process is not necessary; and

YES, I should disregard those processes, myths, and colleges that do not respect the dignity of my studenthood; and

YES, I will not play the "games-R-us" college application racket; and

YES, I do not need to succumb to the "scores-R-us" mentality; and

YES, the benefits of education are well known yet tough to measure; and

YES, no admission officer is going to tell me what I am worth— only I have the power to do that; and

YES, my educational success depends on my own self-confidence. I am going to relax, slow down, take a deep breath, and believe in myself.

Amen.

What can parents do?

Parents, now it is our turn...and what a turn we have already taken. Many critics see a connection between record student stress levels and parental attitudes and behaviors regarding college admissions. In fact, we parents may be as much responsible for contributing to the commercial frenzy surrounding college admissions as anyone else, maybe more. If that is true, what have we learned from reading these essays? What are our educational values, how do we model them, and how do they jibe with studenthood? Finally, what can we do to help our students resist commercial pressures and to derive useful educational benefits from the college planning process?

"I find myself thinking that if students were only left more to their own devices, the process would proceed more appropriately." writes Bill Shain. Michael Thompson, a clinical psychologist who often works with families suffering through college admissions has remarked, "College admissions is infected by irrational forces....It can make normal people act quite nutty, and nutty people act quite crazy." And while admission deans throughout the country compete with colleagues for cocktail hour laughs by comparing "most obnoxious parent" stories, high school counselors and psychologists are painfully recognizing the damaging symptoms of misguided parental pressure.

Stress levels among college-bound students are at all-time highs, and so are parental expectations. One concerned essayist writes, "The pressure can be relentless, even from well–intentioned parents." Dr. Levine, president of Columbia University's Teachers College, recounts an interaction with a student who felt devastated because she had only been admitted to the University of Chicago, Wesleyan, and Swarthmore: "What kind of world is it in which a child who achieves that kind of success feels like a failure? This is so damaging for kids." (*The Christian Science Monitor,* December 2, 2002).

Sometimes in our zeal to help our children gain advantage, we are unwittingly jeopardizing the intended outcome of college admissions—positive admission decisions. Responding to what she describes as, "bad parent etiquette," MIT's Dean of Admission, Marilee Jones, suggests that parents should back off. In recent speeches and writings, she has cited many examples of how parental efforts to help in the admission process have backfired by not allowing the student to come through. "Parents are out of control," Ms. Jones said recently while addressing a group of parents (*Boston Globe,* November 24, 2002).

Well, parents, can we recognize our tendencies to what Washington Post writer Jay Mathews calls, "Ivyholism…an addiction to the notion that brand name colleges make a difference"? Why does it matter whether we get a knock-out rear window decal with our kid's college acceptance? Why do soccer field (and cocktail party) conversations always devolve into chatter about name-brand colleges? There seems to be a certain irony, some observers say, in watching baby boomers obsess over external markers for their children. After all, aren't we the generation that questioned materialism and rejected conformity? I recall receiving an engraved graduation party invitation from a parent. Inside it proudly proclaimed "Come help celebrate: Jon was admitted to the following colleges…" Ugh!

Here are the facts. As parents, it is indeed tough to resist getting over-involved in our children's lives. It is easy to want them to avoid making the mistakes we made, to benefit from our experiences and wisdom, to achieve those things we would want for ourselves, and to verify our success as parents by their own high achievements. And how do we measure these things? You got it; more often than not, we rely on external, commercially derived measurements, such as rank, prestige, popularity, and status—qualities that are easy to grasp and market. Well, easy is not always right, especially when it comes to education. And when it comes to our children's education, we need to recognize the importance of respecting their studenthood, even if this means struggling with our own selfish impulses. Parents, it is not about us.

Most fundamentally, we must abandon the false notion that getting into a brand name college somehow guarantees success. It does not. A study by a Mellon Foundation researcher and a Princeton University economist concludes that student characteristics, such as persistence, curiosity, attitude, etc., determine future earnings, not the college a student attends; that elite individuals, not elite colleges, make for successful futures; that it is what you do—not where you go—that makes the biggest difference in the value of a college experience. A corollary to this notion comes from Nicholas Lemann's book, *The Big Test*, in which the author refers to people who attend the best known schools as Mandarins. Mandarins have their place in society, mostly as technicians and consultants and skilled professionals. They are very good at discerning the rules and carrying out their assignments. However, quite often Mandarins are not the people who make a difference, who create new companies or change minds or establish trends. Those who do, Lemann calls the "Talents." Talents don't need high SAT scores, good extracurricular activities, a dynamite essay, or a prestigious highly-ranked college to make their mark.

Now, listen to Bruce Poch, vice president and dean of admission at Pomona College, as he warns parents about the dangers of inviting commercial involvement in managing our students' college planning: "…consumer warning labels about…college admissions could fill a substantial volume by itself…solutions always require work, not the quick handing over of responsibility for the process to a third party. Know that." And then he amplifies his warning: "They (students) have learned to become supplicants rather than applicants. They can lose their soul in the process or, in what may be even more frightening to the obsessed parent, they may lose their appeal to admissions officers at many colleges because they have homogenized and pasteurized themselves.…"

Those parents still considering investing in commercial college planning services for their students might be wise to recall Karl Furstenberg, Dartmouth's Dean of Admissions, comment about the importance of discerning intrinsic talents when evaluating prospective students. He writes, "The consideration of background factors has become increasingly important precisely because of the way in which commercial college planning services have entered in as a confounding factor.…Stories of $100 per hour counselors sculpting 'kids' resumes abound.…The prevalence of coaching and other services that prepare students for the admission process are a reality which cannot be ignored by admission committees."

A proper appreciation for the student's role in making education happen prepares us for an appropriate roll as parents in the college planning process.

Things for parents to consider:

- Consider that gaming the system may not only diminish your child's studenthood and self-confidence, but it may also jeopardize desired admission outcomes.

- Read and discuss these essays with your child. What are the important messages? Do you agree? Disagree? Why?

- Determine and discuss your family's values about education. What does it mean to be educated? What are the ingredients of good education?

- Identify and evaluate commercial influences in college admissions.

- Limit television watching.

- Discuss the idea of education as an ongoing process, and how selecting a college might be different from buying a stereo.

- Understand that the success of a student's college application process is directly proportional to that student's involvement in the process, and inversely proportional to your involvement. The less you do for the student, the more they do for themselves, and the more successful they will be.

- Eat dinner together as often as possible, but avoid talking about college during dinner!

- Attempt to engage your child in conversation without being intrusive.

- Ask what is important to them in selecting a college and why.

- Select happy, successful friends and ask where they went to college.

- Trust your student enough to allow them to make mistakes.

- Let your student know you are there to help, not to control.

- Try to guide, not push.

- Listen to, encourage, and believe in your child, and be involved with the college planning process but not in control of it.

- Know that applying to college is a warm-up process for college.

- Learn to read your student's body language.

- Help your student develop some ground rules for college admissions. What is a reasonable number of colleges to apply to? What are reasonable selection criteria? How much can parents afford to pay? What is the student's financial obligation?

- Develop a healthy, family-appropriate approach to college admissions that resists commercial attempts to turn the process into a status competition.

- Do not do for your students what they are capable of doing for themselves.

- Resist living vicariously through your student.

- Realize that from the moment we bring our children into the world, we are preparing them to leave us. The college planning process is a training ground for them to practice that.

- Love them enough to let them demonstrate the independence you have instilled in them—and you will be surprised what a testimony they will be to your love.

- Allow your child to own the admission process. If you find yourself wanting to order college applications, fill out college applications, register for SATs or ACTs for your child using the term "we" as in "we are applying to…"; comparing where your child is applying to where your friends' children are applying; overemphasizing numbers, such as test scores and grades; or broadcasting your child's test scores—ask yourself why these would need publicity/publicizing.

Finally, being a student today is different than it was thirty years ago. (This is true even though our kids often say it is!) One of the most obvious differences is the pervasive commercial forces aimed at our children. Or, as one teacher bluntly put it, "Kids these days have so much crap slung at them, it is amazing they are able to survive." So it seems to me that as parents, we need to be especially sensitive to these influences: the role of image, the influence of brand, the bombardment of fast-paced, sound bite information delivery, the amount of time students spend in front of screens, the commercially franchised role of organized competitive sports, the little time our students have to play freely and think and wonder, and the tyranny of having so many choices. These influences contribute to today's students being more anxiety-ridden and more stressed out than any preceding generation. "Taking time out for talk, for play, for a walk, or to join a parent in the kitchen can help a student relax, regroup, and cope," writes Bill Mayher in his excellent book, *The College Admissions Mystique*. With proper perspective, today's parents have a special opportunity to help today's students resist the many anti-educational commercial influences, and to help them take charge of their educational destinies.

Perhaps the most effective inoculation against inappropriate parental involvement is listening to well-wrought advice from veteran parents. What follows is the collective wisdom of fifteen parents who spent more than one hundred years ushering twenty-four children through the college admission process and beyond. Most of these students attended highly selective colleges.

FROM PARENTS TO PARENTS

- Be prepared for frustration, disappointment, learning, and surprises.

- There is no such thing as the "one perfect college."

- What you discover is often better than what you planned.

- What you want for your kid might not be the best for him or her.

- Your kid has to identify and follow his own dream, not the parents' dreams.

- Letting the kid take complete ownership of the process is the best advice.

- If you truly want your kid to be happy, you will let go of your pride over where he goes to college.

- The peer pressure among our schools' parents is far too intense; get real, lighten up, become non-judgmental, and you will be happier as well.

- This process is hardly scientific and predictable; three of our kids went to the same college and each found it to be as different as could be.

- Over-rating our kids can be most damaging to them.

- Be very sensitive to what your kid is communicating through attitude, actions/inactions, and words.

- Believe and trust in your kids.

- It is not the end of the world if a kid changes colleges.

- It takes an unrealistic leap of maturity for 11th and 12th graders to plan their futures.

- Allow this process to be an educational one, filled with discovery, excitement, and faith.

What can colleges do?

"Because colleges are not simply businesses but rather institutions held in trust, it is especially important that their policies are capable of surviving examination by their constituencies."
Michael McPherson and Morton Schapiro, former college presidents and authors, *The Student Aid Game*, 1998.

"Colleges have responsibility for much of the hype that has led to anxiety of all sorts about the admissions process."
Bruce Poch, Vice President and Dean of Admissions, Pomona College.

There are many things colleges could do to reduce commercial interference in the admissions process, and in turn, improve the educational relevance of college admissions. However, the distance between possibility and probability is vast—closing it will be a measure of will power. College leaders first need to recognize that doing the right thing is in their best interest. Then they must be motivated by that call to leadership. Colleges occupy prominent positions in society, and the crisis in college admissions is, in part, a consequence of a growing reluctance on the part of colleges to exercise the public influence entrusted to them. The number of institutional leaders who are pleased with commercial influences in college admissions seems as small as the number of attempts made by leaders to resist these influences. However, such attempts are essential.

James Freedman exhorts college presidents to act beyond institutional self-interest: "For a college president, few opportunities are more rewarding than to be an advocate for liberal education—something this country needs more urgently than it has for some time" (*Liberal Education in the Public Interest*). Enforcing his appeal, he quotes a journalist from *The New York Times*: "A generation ago college and university presidents cut striking figures on the public stage. Today, almost no college or university president has spoken out significantly…about dozens of…issues high on the national agenda." This book, *College Unranked*, is providing an opportunity for college officials to speak out. Here are the voices of discontent, and we present their appeal as a collective conscience.

Before offering a few recommendations, we might do well to consider what Mary Sue Coleman, president of the University of Michigan, writes about James Freedman: "He challenges us to use our offices to defend higher education…to take principled positions on issues of morality, and to inspire our students to change the world." Accordingly, the following recommendations to colleges will be useful so long as the call of conscience and the challenge of providing essential leadership are compelling:

- Recognize that the invasion of commercial values is a problem of significant educational magnitude.

- View this problem as an opportunity to provide essential educational vision and leadership.

- Understand that colleges have the power and obligation to impact education.

- Recommit your institution to serving its public-interest mission.

- Move beyond business models for defining success, determining policies, and demonstrating leadership.

- Cooperate with other institutions in developing a campaign to assert and promote common educational values against divisive commercial practices; embrace the challenge to elevate and distinguish higher education beyond market mechanisms; work to establish collective educational authority in resisting inappropriate commercial influences in education.

- Create alternative mechanisms to the rankings for providing public scrutiny of higher education.

- Establish guiding principles for serving the educational needs of students, as suggested by the discussion of studenthood in this book.

- Invent ways to acknowledge and foster those essential aspects of education that are being diminished by commercialism. For example, instead of enrollment management to serve institutional self-interest, develop "educational management" to promote and serve students' best interests.

- Resist complicity with the rankings. Resist the allure of reputation and status when making important institutional decisions. Resist the drive to continually increase numbers, such as GPAs, SATs, etc.

- Identify educationally questionable practices at your campus and evaluate each practice according to true educational principles—work to disarm these inappropriate practices.

- Consider saying "no" to early decision, merit scholarships, comparisons with other colleges, and the allegiance to selectivity and yield.

- Know that the things that matter in education do not lend themselves to simple scales, hierarchies, ratios, and comparisons; find ways of celebrating these things.

- Let honesty, accuracy, accountability, and consistency guide the selecting, assembling, and reporting of information to all constituents.

- Evaluate the overall educational impact of standardized tests: what are the costs and benefits, and what is the most responsible educational stance?

- Make sure your admission officers are counselors, not sales people.

- Stop treating students as customers by telling them what they want to hear and instead develop policies that treat them as students. Establish admissions as education, not commercialism.

- Be aware that commercialism impairs colleges' abilities to perform a most vital admission function: keeping the playing field level for all applicants. It advantages the well-informed, connected students.

- Avoid the tendency to institutional pretense by publicly acknowledging that the role of the student in the education equation is more significant than the role of the individual college; the student makes the biggest difference.

- Evaluate your college's relationship with The College Board.

- Recognize that guiding students is a trust of great importance and too many adults are violating that trust.

- Allow institutional self-awareness to supplant popularity in securing institutional confidence.

- Stop the admissions arms race.

Some of these suggestions have come directly from our essayists; some are logical derivatives. Clearly, these essays call for leadership, and it is a call offered by those who can help provide such.

Had students or parents been invited to submit essays, there would certainly be an impressive list of recommendations directed at colleges. As expected, the two essays by people in charge of counseling students in the college planning process are especially provocative in their criticisms of colleges. From where these two essayists sit, looking into the eyes of anxious students, they are deeply frustrated with the lack of educational leadership in college admissions. Sean Callaway believes that colleges have a moral responsibility to resist applying inappropriate market techniques to education and to recognize that there are inherent contradictions between various commercially derived practices and educationally determined purposes. He calls on colleges to exercise their obligatory moral leadership by abandoning the rankings. He identifies a small group of colleges as having the power to significantly discredit the rankings by not cooperating with the ranksters. He believes that such collective action would generate "public relations momentum…by promoting education rather than commercialization," and that this momentum would force higher education to "give some important moral example about priorities."

Similarly inspired by his direct work with students, Mark Speyer also calls for responsible behavior among colleges. "It is a fundamental principal of ethics and of law," he writes, "that people are responsible for the predictable consequences of their actions." Colleges must recognize that they define and influence educational standards and that colleges have contributed to the problem by cooperating with the rankings and The College Board, by incessantly competing with each other and pursuing the more-applications-is-better approach to admissions, by focusing on numbers and status as indicators of educational quality, by manipulating numbers to influence rank, and by overemphasizing the importance of SATs. Accordingly, colleges should work to develop and promulgate more intelligent admission standards and more appropriate admission practices than the ones we have now.

A story told by a former vice-president of The College Board now seems prophetic. The scene was a College Board Trustee meeting regarding the Board's new corporate direction. A freshly recruited strategic expert had just completed a presentation promoting a move into the arena of enrollment management. A trustee of the Board who was also a college president expresses concern, "So, you are giving us the tools to carve each other up."

Here we are, drawn to the expanding disconnect between educational purposes and admission practices—a disconnect characterized by commercial interference, denounced by many involved in its creation, and perpetuated by a lack of educational leadership. With little evidence that the billions of dollars diverted to commercial activities have had any educational pay-off, and much more evidence to the contrary, are we now to turn away, again? What would be the price of such continued neglect?

"I do believe that the battle in and for the soul of the university is really one battle in the larger struggle over what values will define American society in the century to come," writes Andrew Delbanco (*The College Board Review*, July 1997). As commercial values and practices begin to dominate college admissions, we can see that there is much at stake. The courage of educational convictions must propel us out of this crisis; inaction is one of the greatest risks to education.

The type of vision necessary to transcend commercial interference receives a prescient clue from the authors of *The Game of Life*, a clue which helps us imagine at least one possible "visionary tactic." Describing the educational perils of appealing to students by telling them what they want to hear, the authors write, "The signals should perhaps be on the side of 'eat your vegetables' instead of 'have some more cake'." Can we notice here a hint that there may be a more appropriate role for marketing in higher education than merely responding to student and parent demand?

Is it possible for higher education to derive educational benefit from certain types of marketing, marketing that says, "This is what we have and this is why you need it," as opposed to, "What do you want? We will give it to you!"

Might higher education be so educationally entrepreneurial as to create demand for real education? Could we at least respect the public's unease about contemporary admissions by offering precepts that are more educationally sensible than the ones currently offered? What we do know is that marketing efforts aimed at meeting students' demands have failed educational purposes. As students, customers cannot and should not always be right. What we have yet to devise is a more powerful and more educationally appropriate marketing campaign, one that responds to the current crisis by reflecting the imagination, creativity, and wisdom so often claimed as the province of higher education. Here may be a challenge worthy of education's most noble intentions: A higher educational role for marketing.

What can The College Board and the media do?

The College Board and members of the media involved with ranking colleges have become big players in the commercial transformation of college admission—big, influential players. Using strategies that seemingly treat students as customers and reduce education to product, both entities have expanded their profits, influence, and stature questionably beyond the boundaries of educational jurisdiction. Most troubling is that their influence appears to be accorded public stature by virtue of business success. There are no meaningful and appropriate mechanisms for public review, input, and restraint—only market mechanisms. The rationale seems to be that if it sells, it must be good for education. And if it can't be sold, who cares?

In 1999, the trustees of The College Board were seeking new leadership—a president to bring needed technological innovation and entrepreneurial savvy to the Board. The trustees found their leader in Gaston Caperton, former governor of West Virginia.

During the ensuing four years, changes at the Board—personnel, policy, products, and revenue—were unprecedented. Mr. Caperton had been effective, but not everyone was pleased. The successful "corporatization" of the Board generated questions about the impact of this success on the educational mission of The College Board. Today, ambivalence and skepticism about the organization continues to emerge—most notably among former Board supporters.

From his vantage point as veteran College Board participant, educator, and admission professional, Ted O'Neill comments on the shift at the College Board by asking: "What happens when we reach a point at which a membership organization is no longer operating in its members' best interests, but rather in its own interests?" Later in his essay, O'Neill allows himself to be more direct: "The marketing of Board products, including tests, undermines the very equity and access the Board promotes." Brad MacGowan, a college counselor and long-time student of College Board policies and practices, describes Board influence and behavior as monopolistic: "The Board has placed and continues to place its own interests and self-perpetuation ahead of students and their education, using aggressive marketing and lobbying with its ownership of the SAT as leverage, to push its products into areas where they are neither helpful nor needed. In short, the Board has become increasingly growth-oriented to the detriment of education, college admissions, and studenthood." A seminal article recently appeared in "National Crosstalk," a publication of the National Center for Public Policy and Higher Education: "Two Faces of the College Board" written by former University of California, Berkeley admission director, Bob Laird. Describing the Board as constantly oscillating between "the magnetic pole of wanting to do good and wanting to do well," Laird, also a former elected officer of the Board, writes: "...now, the needle has swung sharply toward achieving maximum revenue, and the Board's venal streak throbs and pulses powerfully....It is a market animal." These are serious concerns expressed by thoughtful and experienced professionals—professionals who believe in the mission of The College Board. Collectively, these concerns seem to beg the question (paraphrasing Andrew Delbanco): "How far can we go in protecting the bottom line before the organization we are serving loses its soul?"

Leaders of the college rankings industry have no qualms about justifying success by traditional business standards. "We are merely giving the people the information they want," responds Robert Morse of *U.S.News & World Report* during a conference of college admission professionals. Again, there seems to be little sensitivity to the educational impact of the product delivered, no educationally appropriate mechanism to monitor value beyond sales, and little conscience other than that expressed through supply and demand.

A most objective review might conclude that, as products, the SAT (and other College Board products) and The College Rankings are neither good nor bad. They have no inherent value; significance is created in the conflict between their intended purpose and their inevitable use. Intended as tools for selecting students and selecting colleges, these products have acquired prescriptive properties of seemingly authoritative proportion—not just for students, but for parents, deans, presidents, university trustees and alumni. Many educators recognize the signs of damage caused by misuse, while evidence regarding educational benefits of these products is sorely lacking. As the success of the rankings and the SAT become mutually reinforcing (that is, colleges seeking higher rankings encourage students to take the test more often), the chance for conscience to assert itself has diminished.

It is beyond the scope of this book to make recommendations to either The College Board or to the ranking industry. There are certainly many well-intentioned and thoughtful people employed by the media and by The College Board—people who seem genuinely interested in education; people who believe that education can be served corporately; people who might even be interested in promoting studenthood. Furthermore, there should be a proper role for the media and for membership organizations in serving the educational needs of students in college admissions. Certainly, no single entity is in charge of allocating educational value and values. But there are also some important questions regarding responsibility and accountability that most educators would agree must continually guide even the best-intentioned among us: How to reconcile the two, often-opposing goals of public service and profit? How to temper the drive to increase the bottom line with the desire to serve education? How to balance economic expedience with educational vision? How to quantify and justify the important education unmeasurables in a business-driven model of success? These questions have challenged our professional ambitions for a long time; they are particularly relevant in today's college admissions crisis. The comment that the mark of a first-rate intelligence is the ability to hold two opposing ideas in mind at the same time, and still retain the ability to function (F. Scott Fitzgerald), is particularly relevant as we contemplate these questions and discern our individual callings in serving studenthood amid commercial influences. In this context, the best this author/editor can offer to members of The College Board and to members of the media is an invitation to think, and a plea to act intelligently and responsibly:

- Think about the ideas and questions raised by the essayists. What can be done to address these concerns?

- Think about studenthood. What are the qualities that make being a student so important? What can be done to celebrate, promote, and serve these qualities?

- Think about marketing in the context of serving studenthood. Are there opportunities to encourage appropriate educational attitudes and behavior such as confidence, curiosity, imagination, reading, writing, and thinking?

- Think about the huge market which is characterized by fear and anxiety and obsession with numbers and gamesmanship—the market hungry for educational relevance.

- Think about your own individual experience with education, your relationship with learning. What can this tell you about the current commercial influences in college admissions?

- Think big; encouraging and creating demand for real education may be our biggest frontier.

- Think about how standardized testing and the rankings have contributed to the health of higher education. THINK HARD AND FAIRLY ABOUT THIS. Where is the evidence?

- Think about the opportunity to improve college admissions in America. What would this take?

- Imagine the popularity of such a campaign!

- Imagine a definition of success which included more than just profit.

- Imagine a college admissions process in which testing and ranking had diminished roles. What would the opportunities be?

- Imagine that there is a role for appropriate educational marketing.

Hope and Inspiration

Good education can connect conscience to leadership. It can make "Do The Right Thing" more appealing than "Just Do It," and help shape a citizenry beyond mere consumer impulses. Dangers arise when market mechanisms and values begin to direct the management of educational institutions. This book, which began as an experiment in detecting educational leadership amid encroaching commercial influences, grew into a project through the courageous responses of college officials. Summoned by concerns beyond institutional self-interest, these voices deserve individual recognition. But it is the combined impact of these insiders' efforts—as they seem to coalesce in a collective conscience—that confronts us, inspires us, and directs us to move beyond commercial interference.

Studenthood, a concept derived in the nucleus of this conscience, has utmost significance. Studenthood embodies education's most precious resource: those qualities which define and give value to being a student. Studenthood draws our attention to the essentiality of these qualities, forcing us to seek educational clarity and directing the development of appropriate standards and practices. Studenthood can provide both the conceptual stability and visionary fortitude to deliver education from commercial interference. It may even inspire collective action. Welcome to the campaign!

Acknowledgements

Many people have made this project possible. Among them, the essayists deserve first mention. Thanks for believing, writers; thank you for your effort and trust. Students I have known over the years also deserve recognition. By sharing your stories and demonstrating the courage to be students amid unfortunate commercial distractions, you have inspired this project. Thanks, students, for being this counselor's reward.

In the "thanks for the encouragement" department, Mike Sexton is a trusted and shrewd personal trainer. I would not have survived round one without him. Jennifer Britz belongs here, too. It was two years ago, following my remarks at a NACAC conference, that the idea for *College Unranked* was conceived high above the Utah plains. "Thacker, you need to write a book," Britz said, as she sat down in the adjacent airline seat and brandished a yellow writing pad. "Start talking." Britz has since become constant confidant, promoter, and participant. And, I cannot forget Jacques Steinberg of *The New York Times*, whose noble interest in this topic has already helped make a difference in college admissions.

So many others have distinguished their professionalism by encouraging me to pursue this controversial project: Paul Stoneham, Paul Driscoll, Matt Fissinger, Karl Furstenberg, Michael Beseda, Ken Skipper, Ted O'Neill, Gyimah Boadi, Bonnie Marcus, Philip Ballinger, Jeff Rickey, Lee Kay, Joe Kertes, Kate Prael, Jon Reider, Margaret Korzus, Frank Sachs, Bruce Poch, Will Dix, Brad MacGowan, Paul Marthers, and Jim Sumner. In various ways, these fine folks have helped me remain standing during the tough times of self-doubt and adversity. Cheers to all of you, and to those I have thoughtlessly forgotten to mention.

Priceless technical support was provided by my editors, Kirsten Leonard and Janice Watson, both of whom provided expertise and inspiration beyond their contractual roles; the creative team of Dawna Allison, Anne Verhoeven, and Loren Leed, that took unusual ownership and performed creative magic with this project; and, of course, Margo Pardee, whose delightful willingness and expert execution had therapeutic effects.

My parents and siblings deserve special tribute, and I mean this most sincerely. Sister Jill, for believing, editing, and suffering my shortcomings without complaint; sister Jane, for her can-do (anything) attitude, accomplishments, and moral support; and sister Judy, for her creativity, interest, resourcefulness, and sensitivity. The three of you have taught me many invaluable lessons. And Barbara and Arn, you created the bliss—an enduring childhood.

The demands of this project created tough personal challenges, and diverted my attention from family. Somehow, I feel inadequate in my attempt to express gratitude to Lori, Sam, and Jake. Perhaps this is testimony to the strength of our bonds.

And finally, to Jim Wolfston, a brilliant and successful businessman who cannot ignore social issues: Thanks for believing and for taking a chance.

Special thanks:

Through the generous support of these Founding Sponsors, The Education Conservancy is able to publish *College Unranked,* and to launch projects that will advance the issues raised in this book.

Bard College

CollegeNET, Inc.

Earlham College

Kenyon College

Lewis & Clark College

Reed College

St. Mary's College of California

University of Chicago

Philip Ballinger

Bonnie Marcus

Ted O'Neill

Jim Wolfston

The Education Conservancy

In February 2004, Lloyd Thacker left high school counseling to establish The Education Conservancy (EC)—a non-profit organization committed to helping students, counselors, and colleges overcome commercial interference in college admissions. By harnessing the involvement, research, and ideas of thoughtful educators, EC is working to deliver appropriate advice, services, and advocacy. The first significant contribution is *College Unranked*.

Advisory Board Members:

Philip Ballinger
Director of Admissions
University of Washington

Paul Marthers
Dean of Admissions
Reed College

Michael Beseda
Vice Provost for Enrollment
St. Mary's College of
California

Ted O'Neill
Dean of Admission
University of Chicago

Jennifer Britz
Dean of Admission
Kenyon College

Jeff Rickey
Dean of Admissions
Earlham College

Bonnie Marcus
Senior Associate Director of
Admissions
Bard College

Mike Sexton
Dean of Admission
Lewis & Clark College

THE EDUCATION CONSERVANCY

805 SW Broadway, Suite 1600, Portland, OR 97205
www.educationconservancy.org
(503) 290-0083